"*At Heaven's Doorway: Mystical Golden Roses for Spiritual Growth* is written on two levels. First we have Diane's CAPTIVATING AND ENTHRALLING memoir. And second, Diane's sharing of her palpable discovery, mission and fulfillment. This reviewer doesn't often use the word "BEAUTIFUL" to describe a book or an author . . . but Diane Line and *At Heaven's Doorway* are beautiful!"

~ Richard Fuller, Senior Editor
Metaphysical Reviews

At Heaven's Doorway

Mystical Golden Roses
for Spiritual Growth

authorHOUSE®

AuthorHouse™
1663 Liberty Drive, Suite 200
Bloomington, IN 47403
www.authorhouse.com
Phone: 1-800-839-8640

This book is a work of non-fiction. Unless otherwise noted, the author and the publisher make no explicit guarantees as to the accuracy of the information contained in this book and in some cases, names of people and places have been altered to protect their privacy.

First published by AuthorHouse 6/5/2008

ISBN: 978-1-4343-3947-8 (sc)
ISBN: 978-1-4343-3946-1 (hc)

Printed in the United States of America
Bloomington, Indiana

This book is printed on acid-free paper.

*Dedicated to the memory of my
grandson, Luke Carrington.*

*He enriched our lives and gave our
hearts love that will last a lifetime.*

ACKNOWLEDGEMENTS

I wish to express my gratitude and heartfelt appreciation to the many people who made this book possible. Without their help and encouragement, this book might never have become a reality:

Barbara Allen, my dearest friend and mentor—special thanks for your love and support through the years.

Ellen, I have not forgotten your willingness to contribute time and effort during those early stages.

My daughter Valerie, with whom sharing spiritual experiences led me to capture their very essence in these pages.

My husband Lloyd, who encouraged me with his continuous love and belief in me.

June Rouse, creative writing teacher and consultant, who guided me to my own clearest voice. Your invaluable advice made this book possible.

Linda Anderson, an infinitely patient advisor.

Kate Robinson, who enjoys assisting her colleagues in realizing their literary dreams.

Mark Johnson and George Barr, research librarians at the Franklin Park, Illinois, Public Library.

And with gratitude for my granddaughters, Alexis Rae—"Lexie"—and Victoria Rose—"Tori"—cherished blessings, and to my Lord, who gave me the opportunity to live at Heaven's doorway.

FOREWORD

There is nothing new about visions, prophecy, healings or dreams. Although many people insist they don't believe in them, I have yet to meet anyone who doesn't seem interested in these subjects.

In 1974, Diane was a student in one of my metaphysical classes for self-hypnosis. During the first few classes, I discovered what a unique individual she is. I knew then we were to share something important.

Over our years of friendship, Diane has confided in me about her abilities and the spiritual events that have happened in her life. In this book, *At Heaven's Doorway*, Diane takes the reader on her spiritual journey. You will see she uses her sixth sense and has a relationship with God that many of us want but aren't able to consciously obtain.

You should understand that the events in Diane's story involve actual people—her loved ones—family, friends, and a few heavenly beings. Many events are verifiable; witnesses confirm that they happened.

Today there are many people aware of forces that interact with our lives, forces that operate in a dimension beyond the knowledge of our five senses. For instance, through Diane's experiences, readers can come to know there is life after what we call death, a life in which the personality of the loved one remains the same, where infants or children grow, and adults have a youthful, healthy look. People either recently or long dead, known as apparitions and not usually visible to the human eye, sometimes become visible to gifted people. Apparitions sometimes speak to and touch the living. These beings have passed into another dimension where they have begun their afterlife. To help us here, some may linger near places that they knew in life. Their spirit bodies may even materialize briefly.

In this book, Diane helps us empathize with the life after death experience through her own personal experiences and those of her daughter, Valerie. She will capture your heart for all time as she shares her spiritual adventure. Knowing Diane as I do, I understand that she wishes others to be as enthralled by those experiences as she was and still is.

I need to speak briefly of Luke Carrington, whom Diane writes about so movingly. Baby Luke was meant to be here only a short time, to brighten the dark corners of every room. He had to be perfect and he was.

Our Lord, the Merciful One, allowed his grief-filled mother to smell the fragrance of roses on baby Luke's shawl when there were no roses nearby. Until one experiences something so magnificent, which happens just for them, they may find it impossible to believe such a thing could happen. I pray that before you go, your eyes will see the glory; your ears will hear the heavenly chords; your heart will be touched by the perfection of tiny baby fingers; and that you will walk on the road of awareness in the great, white, bright light of God's love that dwells deep inside us all.

My pride is great for Diane; we are truly sisters of the spirit on a very special journey. I wrap you, Diane, in your tapestry of a well-loved life, a life I am fortunate to be part of and will continue to share.

My sister, my special friend, I love you.

Bright blessings,
Barbara Allen, M.A.

PREFACE

I never planned to write a memoir, nor did I intend to be an instrument of God's will. But both happened. It would have been easier for me to hide in my own little corner of the world rather than write this book. In experiencing the events chronicled here and writing about them, my daughter Valerie and I learned everyone has a purpose to fulfill, no matter how limited our lives may seem.

I shed many tears as I reflected on my memories while writing this book. I learned how the ordinary becomes extraordinary, how love reaches beyond death, and how invisible beings influence lives. By reading my story, you may discover solutions to mysteries in your own lives. As with many books, however, the greater message is found between the lines.

It is not my intention to change your beliefs about your faith, but rather to strengthen your love of God. I realize what I have written may be somewhat startling and possibly unbelievable. Yet my narrative is true, no matter how incredible it may sound.

Diane

CONTENTS

ACKNOWLEDGEMENTS VII
FOREWORD by Barbara Allen IX
PREFACE by Diane Line XI
1   THE GOLDEN ROSE 1
2   THE DOORWAY 13
3   MY MENTOR 23
4   THE AWAKENING 31
5   PORTALS OF DREAMS 37
6   CONQUERING EVIL 45
7   HEAVEN IS ON MY SIDE 53
8   THE VISIT 57
9   IN THE PALM OF HIS HAND 63
10   THE CHRISTMAS ANGEL 69
11   A JOB WELL DONE 79
12   MY GUARDIAN ANGEL 87
13   THE SPIRITUAL HEART 93
14   AN ANGEL AMONG US 101
15   THE CHERUB 109
16   A GIFT FROM LUKE 113
17   HEARTSTRINGS FROM HEAVEN 121
18   LITTLE SNOWFLAKE 125
19   VALERIE'S ENLIGHTENMENT 129
20   THE SPIRITUAL HEALINGS 137
21   AT HEAVEN'S DOORWAY 143
LYRICS: *Because* 147
EPILOGUE 149
CHAPTER NOTES 151

You are a child of the universe

CHAPTER ONE:
THE GOLDEN ROSE

A spiritual purpose is revealed through the
cross and a golden rose

In early 1994, I spent many hours consoling my daughter Valerie after the death of her baby son, Luke Carrington. Luke's death had been difficult for all of us to accept, especially his mother. Her long, naturally curly cinnamon-colored hair drooped around her face and the vacant place behind her deep blue eyes touched me every time we were together. She was expecting another baby in late April; still, her grieving continued.

I began writing in a journal to relieve the pressure of Valerie's grief and the loss of my first grandchild. We experienced many supernatural phenomena such as guardian angel interventions, visions of spirits, and heavenly forces that guided our lives and reassured us of God's love. After a year and a half of comforting her, I fell deathly ill myself.

For the previous five years, I'd worked as a recreational therapist for a community hospital outside Chicago, Illinois. One morning as I walked across the hospital parking lot and onto the sidewalk, a gripping fear surrounded me. A block away from the hospital, I gasped, desperate to take another breath. The wind chill factor had dipped to a dangerous fifty degrees below zero and the extreme cold aggravated my asthma. Inside the hospital entrance, I began breathing easier and when I composed myself, I went upstairs. On Saturday mornings I was expected to conduct the prayer service for the patients on the skilled-care unit.

During the morning break, I looked into the mirror and noticed that my porcelain complexion had darkened to a medium brown. I knew something was terribly wrong. I called my husband to see if he could drive me home after he'd finished work. Lloyd agreed with a deliberate gentlemanly air, but he wasn't available until the end of my shift. I managed to start the prayer service until a concerned patient noticed how ill I was and asked to read from the *Lutheran Digest*. Relieved, I sat and watched, realizing I was too sick to work.

I called Lloyd again after the prayer service ended. I decided to drive myself home, unaware my lungs were shutting down from a combination of asthma and a severe respiratory flu, a life-threatening condition.

To relieve my headache, I leaned back in the seat and laid my head against the neck rest as I drove home from the hospital. I was thinking of our little sweetheart, six-and-a-half-month old Luke. He had died over a year ago from a sudden bout of bacterial meningitis. I reminisced about my grandmother and parents caring for me at the two-story house where I grew up on Octavia Street in Chicago. Grandma Verda, my mother's mother, heard me whimpering, sick with a bout of Asian flu, from her apartment below us. She climbed the eighteen stairs to my parents' apartment unaided.

Several years before, she was injured in a car accident that left her legs rigid. In order to climb any staircase, she leaned to the left side of the banister, holding the rail and placing the crutch against the wall into the seam of the next stair. Then she placed her right foot onto the stair and lifted herself up. For years, my step-grandfather Harry was right behind her when she ascended or in front of her when she descended the staircase. Her climb upstairs to care for me was a difficult and gallant act, and since her death, a constant inspiration to me.

That day, Grandma Verda and I were alone in the two-story house. My mom, dad and grandfather were working. I was in the kitchen removing ice from a tray when Grandma Verda walked up behind me. She placed her arm around my waist.

"What's wrong, Diane?" she asked, concerned.

Surprised, I didn't answer her question right away. Instead, I turned from the counter to face her.

"How did you get up here?"

"I heard you crying, sweetheart. What's wrong?"

"I don't feel good. I have this terrible headache. It feels like a hammer is hitting the top of my head."

"Diane, come downstairs so I can take care of you until your parents come home from the restaurant. I've changed the sheets on the bed in the front bedroom today; it's all ready for you."

With a slight smile, Grandma Verda patted my left arm, turned as she held the edge of the counter, and wobbled across the kitchen. I noticed her crutch against the doorway and yelled out to her.

"Grams, do you need your crutch?"

"No, dear, bring it with you when you come downstairs."

The following morning, before my parents rode together to their restaurant in Franklin Park, my mom cooked and served me breakfast. Before they left, they both stood by the doorway and visited with me. By the third day, I went back upstairs to finish recuperating, going downstairs only when Grandma called me for dinner.

One night that same week, my Dad came home early from the restaurant. My mother was at her professional businesswomen's meeting. I noticed when she left she was dressed in a new tan suit with gold and brown beads at the shoulders. A cocoa brown pillbox hat, brown alligator shoes, purse, and a pair of brown kid gloves matched her attire. She polished her appearance with a fox stole over her suit jacket. Her bright, Technicolor red hair, perfectly coiffed in curls and waves, accented her gorgeous complexion. She was lovely and at the height of professional perfection.

Later that night, I walked into the kitchen and stood next to the table where Dad occasionally typed the restaurant menu specials on my portable typewriter. He looked up at me when I entered the room. A handsome man of Anglo-Saxon heritage, he had dark brown hair parted in the center with natural waves on either side and a small brown mustache that tickled and sometimes poked when he kissed me.

"Ye . . . ss?" he said dramatically, with expression.

"Dad, do you remember when I was born?"

"I remember it well. I had a gig with the band that evening at Broadway and Lawrence Avenue. I arrived at the hospital after you were born, about 3:30 in the morning. I visited with your mother for a few minutes and told her I'd come back the next day. Then I gave her a kiss for doing a good job having you. A nurse asked me to follow her to the nursery where I could see you through the window in your bassinet. You were real small. One of your eyes was shut and your head came to a point at the top."

"Is that true?" I squealed.

"Yes, it's true. I didn't know what to think. I left the nursery window wondering if you were going to look like that or grow out of it."

"Which eye was open?"

"I don't remember. I think your left eye. I wouldn't worry about it, Diane. You turned out to be a pretty baby. For a few years while you were growing and in puberty, you were an ugly duckling with your weight out of control, glasses, and corrective shoes for turned-in toes. But look at you now—a flawless complexion, large blue-grey eyes like your mother, a tantalizing shape and a good-humored personality."

"That part must be like you, huh?" I mocked, thinking how similar our personalities were.

"Do you know what you symbolized at birth?" Notoriously over-dramatic, Dad sometimes used philosophical references while telling jokes.

I smirked. "I don't know if I want to hear this."

Dad ignored my remark. "I read in the newspaper that on the reverse side of the dollar bill is an unfinished pyramid and a capstone with the Eye of Providence in the center."

"What's that?"

"The presence of a divine spirit watching over us."

"But, Dad. It's on a pyramid."

"Yes. The pyramid of Giza in Egypt, I believe. Did you know there is a small, mysterious shaft going up to the pyramid's peak, pointing toward stars that never disappear in the sky?"

"Dad, the Egyptians believe in sun gods and other gods."

"Yes, they did. They were from another time and culture, but they had one thing in common with us. They believed in a higher

4

power and the divine spirit in all things. Most religions are based on this principle, yet for centuries wars have been fought because people could not tolerate each others' beliefs. Promise me, Diane, you'll always respect the different faiths and practices of others."

"You thought all that when you looked at me?"

"Well, not exactly." He paused, then continued. "The only way I could comprehend your pointed head and one eye staring at me was to believe they were symbols of some kind. I never forgot that look."

"But, what does it mean for me?"

"I don't know. Maybe nothing. I guess we'll just have to wait and see."

When I returned home from the hospital, I changed into a fresh nightgown and climbed into bed. I thought I was falling into a light sleep, but I was actually slipping through Heaven's doorway into a near-death experience. Suddenly I saw the spirit of my deceased grandmother hovering over me.

I smiled. She climbed the stairs for me again, I thought. Breathless, I lifted my head off the pillow and whispered, "Grams, I'm dying."

Beyond my grandmother, three women dressed in black mourning clothes stood at the bedroom doorway. I glanced up at them, too sick to speak. I rolled over and dozed off again.

I awoke unexpectedly and found myself standing in a garden near a tree covered in pink wild roses. Beyond me lay a dirt path with tall grass growing on either side. I took a tentative step and started down the path. In the distance, the outline of a small, ivory-colored village hovered on the horizon.

When I arrived at the village entrance, the exalted form of Jesus Christ stood on a platform, wearing a white linen robe and brown leather sandals. My attention centered on the illuminating light radiating from His body. He came down the stairs and greeted me with a smile. I couldn't believe He was walking toward me.

"Lord," I cried.

He cupped my face with the palms of His hands and looked into my eyes. "You are a child of the light."

"Did I die, Lord?"

"No, you haven't died. Come, we have something for you." He directed me to a white, wooden doorway.

The huge doors opened, revealing rows of long, polished, wooden pews in a simple, light-colored room. Deceased friends and relatives rose and greeted us, applauding. They were dressed in clothing they had worn during their earthly lives.

My parents walked toward us; they appeared younger and healthier than I remembered them in life. My mother looked lovely in a long, gold-trimmed white gown. At first, I couldn't comprehend that my parents were in spirit form until I noticed Mom wearing the same gown she described in a prophetic dream she had when I was a young girl.

"Mom, you look *good*. Heaven certainly agrees with you."

"I liked what you wrote about me. You make me sound so beautiful."

She can talk again, I thought, surprised. The tone of her voice had softened and with improvements in her health, her personality had changed for the better.

As we gathered in a circle, Christ called my parents by their first names.

"Ed, how proud you must be of Diane," He said.

Dad, handsome in the white tuxedo jacket, black trousers and bow tie that he'd worn on my wedding day, smiled back at the Lord.

"Oh, Dad, if I'd known, I would have brought a bottle to toast this occasion," I said, remembering how Dad had enjoyed alcohol at festivities.

"Diane, there's no desire here for drinking or smoking," he replied. While alive, alcohol had been his addiction and in the end, it killed him. In his new life, the craving no longer existed.

By now, I assumed the room was one of Heaven's meeting halls. Christ nodded to my parents, directing me to the front of the room toward a stage, empty except for a simple podium and a big-band orchestra accented by a large maroon swag. I couldn't help recalling how I'd struggled to remember the words from the big band music of Dad's era.

Christ directed me to stand next to Him in the center of the stage. "I'm so pleased with what you've written in your journal and all you've accomplished. Your story is like no other. You have blended many levels of spirituality, using them skillfully in your own life. And you have also helped strengthen your daughter's spiritual growth." He put his arms around me. "No one can ever hurt you again. You have written for the entire world from your heart and your heart is beautiful."

Christ walked to the podium at the front of the stage. He began to speak with an air of leadership in a warm tone, generating love toward everyone. Several times during the ceremony, He turned to smile at me and asked the others to pray for my work. He spoke of His love for me and all humanity.

The large double doors suddenly opened and a graceful woman glided toward the stage. Her luminous face was more delicate than any I'd ever imagined. Her features radiated an indescribable purity and sweetness. In awe, I nodded and smiled at her, and she returned the gesture.

Christ turned from his audience. "Diane, My mother would like to give you something."

Mary looked directly at me, her eyes penetrating mine. "I will pray for you. Soon the world will know about you and how you were chosen. Thank you for helping my son reach the world."

She handed a small, golden globe to me. As it touched my palm, it opened into several leaf-like parts resembling a flower. At the center stood a long-stemmed golden rose. My attention focused on the slightly bent stem and on the mysterious light radiating from Mary to me. She took the rose from the center of the globe and held it next to my clothing. Deep warmth penetrated my chest cavity when she laid it directly over my heart. At that, the sphere's petals closed, and with her hands over mine, we held the small globe together.

Christ stood beside us, speaking words of thanksgiving and new hope for the world. He blessed us with tiny white doves that flew above our heads. Mary moved to the other side of the stage. As she faded from my view, the center doors opened again. A procession of saints filled the room. I recognized only a few from pictures I'd seen.

Saint Joan of Arc was the first to enter. She appeared small, boyishly dressed in a military uniform. I'd always admired her strength of courage and determination to lead others in what she believed to be right.

The Apostles were next, followed by the beautiful Saint Bernadette Soubirous. They formed a line on the stairs leading up to the stage. I approached them and we greeted each other. They told me their names, then explained their life's work and why they wanted to meet me.

I paused in front of Saint Bernadette Soubirous. More petite than I'd imagined, and though dressed in peasant clothing, she was lovely. She referred to my asthma and spoke about the suffering of all who live on earth. She told me she'd learned to love suffering, because it brought her nearer to God.

The doors opened again and Mother Mary, in the form of the Virgin of Guadalupe, made her entrance. Her beauty, accented by rays of light radiating from her, dazzled me. She wore a green cloak dotted with gold stars, held in place by a gold crown. Her red dress had an embossed design that matched the single golden rose she carried. Her feet did not touch the floor; rather, she seemed to float toward the stage. As she passed in front of me, she bowed her head and smiled, then disappeared and reappeared on the other side of the room.

Christ directed me to sit on the steps in front of the podium. When I'd done so, He said, "Diane, we wish to extend our deep gratitude."

My attention turned to the choir loft directly above the center doors. My father sang the first few bars of a popular song familiar to me. In the center of the ceiling hovered twenty cherubs dancing in various positions while building a large matrix. The rotating movement within each group formed a kaleidoscopic pattern of uniquely shaped crystals.

Through one of the prisms, I caught a glimpse of my grandson's enchanting face. He had inherited our Scots-Irish complexion and glow of high color, the large blue eyes, and the hint of red hair prominent through the generations in my mother's family. He sat perched on the railing of the balcony to the right of my dad, while cherubs in front of them harmonized to the strains of the song *Because*.

Overwhelmed by the beauty of the prismatic colors, I listened, spellbound, to the music's melodic harmonies. Grandeur beyond description, it heightened my sense of sight, touch and hearing. Tears of spiritual bliss ran down my face. I realized Heaven was healing me through my senses. I remembered how I'd used soothing sounds on my own patients to ease their pain. Now Heaven used a combination of energies to heal me.

As the music's final bars echoed above me, trumpets sounded behind me. I rose on the steps in front of the podium and turned toward the stage. Two angels stood on each side of the orchestra, playing the introduction from Handel's *Messiah.*

God, the Lord of Lords, walked toward the center of the stage dressed in iridescent robes resembling the shimmer of opals, trimmed in gold and outlined in diamonds, pearls, rubies, crystals and other precious stones. A matching headdress studded with jewels crowned His head. Two cherubs hovering in mid-air lifted his matching cloak behind Him. He shimmered with a magnificent radiance.

"I have called you by name. You have done what I have asked of you. Today you receive the highest gift Heaven gives to an earth angel. You will share your life, choosing to light the world for the sake of humanity. You are a true philanthropist. Child of light, you never thought yourself intelligent enough, wealthy enough or beautiful enough to write. Have I not provided these things for you? And when the greed of others hurt you, did I not give back what was taken? Did you not prosper?"

The beauty of His majestic presence overwhelmed me. My dry throat rendered me speechless. As tears filled my eyes, I smiled at Him and nodded.

He walked toward me at the front of the stage and whispered softly. "Don't worry. When people read the words in your book, they will know you have seen and heard Me."

I felt His love wrap around my spirit and become part of me. Christ extended his hand and guided me down the stairs. I turned to God to thank Him, but He was no longer there. We strolled toward the opened doors where thousands stood waiting for us.

"You will help all of them." Christ pointed to the gathered crowd.

Outside, people lined each side of the path, cheering and applauding as I walked by. When I reached the wild rose tree, I turned around. Christ stood with my family, smiling and waving at me.

I smiled and waved good-bye. Lloyd called me from a distance. "Diane, Diane. Are you all right?"

I didn't want to answer him.

Ever since the near-death experience, I can see the afterglow of God's light in photographs of me. So many pictures of me were developed with spots of light that I finally realized this phenomenon was a result of my near-death experience.

I related my discovery to my friend and mentor, Barbara Allen, in one of our monthly cassette tape exchanges.

"Diane, do you remember when I told you about the afterglow?" she replied. "You do know all who have experienced a near death are given the afterglow of light from the creator. That's why people mention the twinkling lights above your head, your light complexion, or the photographs with dots around your face."

She continued. "You'll have to come to terms with the fact that you're an earth angel and have a job to do. Allow nothing to stand in the way of dedicating yourself to the universe." She signed off at the end of the tape in a soothing voice. "Pax and Bright Blessings."

"Everything is in divine order," I said softly.

There were two things I couldn't explain as I reflected on all that had happened when I walked through Heaven's Doorway: the two enactments of the Virgin Mother and the golden rose.

After I recovered from the severe respiratory flu that led to my near-death experience, I telephoned my brother-in-law, Bobby. He'd recently visited the Virgin of Guadalupe Shrine in Mexico City. I asked him if a golden rose was in the shrine.

He thought for a moment. When I mentioned that the rose had a slightly bent stem, he grew excited. "Yes, there is a golden rose lying next to a gold cross in the old basilica," he said. "You've never seen the shrine so you'll need to imagine how it looks. There are tunnels with plates hanging on the walls, covered with thank you notes from people who've had miracles granted to them. In a clearing, the golden rose and the gold cross lay under glass. I believe the rose was a gift from a Pope to the Virgin of Guadalupe. There's a story about the rose," he explained. "Years ago, some banditos wanted to destroy the shrine, so they placed a bomb in the basilica. When the bomb exploded, the rose became bent, but the church was unharmed."

After Bobby told me this story, my near-death experience took on new meaning. I started analyzing the legend of the golden rose at the shrine and the symbol of the golden rose in my experience. Perhaps, I speculated, Mary had appeared to me as the Virgin of Guadalupe so that I'd be able to understand the significance of the golden rose she had given me.

As I reflected on the words of Jesus and Mary, I grew to understand that my heart signified my life story and that the golden rose Mary placed over my heart represented God's spiritual protection.

When God's divine doorway opens you'll find Heaven in your heart, for His kingdom is within. His presence guides my life and I offer my heart to the entire world.

CHAPTER TWO:
THE DOORWAY

A spiritual doorway connects Heaven and Earth

In January of 1971, my mom telephoned me from the V.A. hospital where my dad was a patient. The doctors decided to discontinue Dad's kidney dialysis treatments when the appearance of another deadly complication had developed.

"Diane, it's not good. The doctor said Dad is having a difficult time breathing with the pneumonia. They're placing him on a respirator in the intensive care unit."

"Oh, no," I exclaimed. "Mom, we'll be right there."

When Lloyd and I arrived at the hospital's intensive care unit, some of my parents' relatives and close friends were gathered in the hallway. A quiet calm filled the air as we greeted each other. Lloyd stood silently next to my father's friend, Joe, while Mom ushered me into the large, dimly lit ward.

The nurse met us inside the doorway of his room. "Be careful of what you say to him," she warned.

"Will he hear us?" I asked.

"He might. Even though he's in a coma, the hearing is the last to shut down." The nurse opened the door to the enclosed entryway of the oldest section of the hospital ward.

Dad was alone, lying on a gurney in the center of the room. Four freestanding floodlights with aluminum shades were shining on him. They reminded me of the lights he used when he made family movies. This time, instead of working behind the camera he was the central figure.

The respirator and heart monitor stood to one side of him. The heavily coated cords from the equipment and the lights lay skewed on the floor around the gurney.

We walked to him. The air rushing into his lungs from the respirator moved his head back with an annoying force.

I placed my hand on his shoulder. "Dad, we're both here."

Mom stood next to me and picked up his hand. "Come on, Ed. You can do it. You can beat this."

"Mom, I think he heard us. Look, there's a tear in his eye. He's trying to say good-bye."

I stepped back and behind them as Mom leaned closer to Dad. She held a handkerchief to his cheek and caught the tear.

While we drove home from the hospital later that night, I silently asked God why He didn't send His angels to help Dad. As Protestants we believed our prayers went directly to God. We believed God sent angels to guide, protect and relay messages to people centuries ago.

Angels appeared in our daily Bible study stories at my Lutheran school. Why didn't we have these miraculous visitations in our lives today? When I was a teen, I finally summoned the courage to ask the question in one of my high school religion classes. Taking a deep breath, I raised my arm.

"Yes, Diane?" the teacher asked.

"Why don't angels appear to help us now, Pastor?"

There was a burst of giggles across the room and the pastor responded with a slight smile. I felt a flush of heat travel up my face as someone whispered, "That's a stupid question."

The pastor, annoyed at what he considered giddiness, tapped his desk with a pen.

"Okay, class. Calm down," he ordered.

Looking directly at me, he answered solemnly. "Diane, angels are messengers. They do what is asked of them through God's will. We don't see angels because they are spirits. You . . . can't . . . see . . . a . . . spirit."

For one brief moment, our eyes met. I looked down and gazed at the desktop and ran my index finger over the deeply engraved letters on the top, God is love . . . God is love.

Logically, I realize that many people don't accept the idea of spirits or heavenly beings coming into our homes to assist us or save us from harm. Twentieth and twenty-first century technology ignited growth in scientific and industrial skills. Gradually the structure of religion changed, creating an intellectual climate not conducive to the existence of angels. My concept of angels was about to change forever as Heaven's invisible world came into my life.

A week after my Dad's funeral, Mom and I returned to the restaurant. Mom had not only lost my father, she'd assumed full responsibility for their business. Managing it had been hard work for two. Now she did it alone, except for what little help I could give her, because Lloyd worked nights and I cared for our seven-year old daughter.

After the New Year, I took down the large Christmas wreath that hung in the restaurant's front window. I put the decorations and ornaments into a box on the storage room shelf and placed the wreath against the wall. After the lunch hour had ended, I went back through the kitchen and into the storage room to get my coat. Mom was sitting at the desk putting payroll checks in envelopes for the employees before they left for the day.

I slipped on my boots and grabbed my long winter coat. "Mom, what are you going to do with the Christmas wreath?"

"Would you mind putting it in the dumpster on your way out?" She handed me a payroll envelope. "It's getting dry, a real fire hazard."

"I was thinking of taking the wreath to the cemetery and putting it on Dad's grave."

"That's a good idea. He loved decorating the restaurant for the holidays and didn't get to see the wreath this year."

Each December, Mom, Dad, Valerie, Lloyd and I helped bring in the holidays by decorating the restaurant for Christmas. We shared love and laughter as we decorated, and it became an annual ritual. Many of the employees stayed to help. Sometimes a customer walking by the large front window waved and stopped in. Then all of us celebrated together.

Lloyd had decorated the front window with little panes he squared off in red tape. Then he sprayed fake snow on the sides of each pane to create drifts. In the center of the window we hung a sparkling, white, flocked wreath decorated with red silk poinsettias and gold ornaments held in place by a large red bow. The Christmas wreath glistened under a spotlight, adding warmth to the restaurant's atmosphere.

I placed the wreath in the trunk of our car and drove to the cemetery. As I got out of the car I noticed no one had visited Dad's grave since the funeral. Only my footprints were visible in the light snow. I laid the wreath on his grave with a prayer.

"This will keep you warm, Dad," I said aloud, referring to the warmth and cheerful hum of the people in the restaurant.

The next day, one of Dad's old songs played in my mind, one he'd taught me as a little girl. He was thanking me for my heartfelt gift through the song's lyrics. This wasn't surprising since my father was a musician and vocalist. What did surprise me was that we could communicate at all! I never thought a spiritual bond could exist after someone died.

One afternoon, several months after Dad's death, Lloyd listened to me singing from the kitchen doorway. He finally asked, "What song are you singing?"

Shaken, I turned from the sink to face him. "You scared me."

He gave me a slight smile. "Well, what song is it?"

I tried to sound casual. "Oh, just one of the old songs my dad recorded. Why?"

"I just wondered. You keep repeating it."

"Oh. Uh . . . well," I stammered, "I'm trying to remember the words, that's all."

The hardest part was trying to figure out the titles and the lyrics of each song that popped into my mind, because it was "his" music from the big band era of the 1930s and 1940s. I dismissed the music playing in my head as a symptom of grief.

"Lloyd, do you think we could take Mom to the cemetery next week? She hasn't been there since Dad died. Maybe we can go out to dinner like we did last year."

"Whatever you want," he said, leaving the decision up to me.

On Palm Sunday in 1971, Lloyd, Valerie, Mom and I drove to the cemetery to visit Dad's grave. A mile from the cemetery, Valerie, who sat next to her grandmother, crawled over the front seat and sat between Lloyd and me.

"Mom, how far is it to Grandpa's grave?"

"We're almost there, Val." I patted her leg.

When we turned into the cemetery, Valerie climbed on my lap to look out the window at the headstones. "Look, there's an angel with a broken wing. There's another one. That one's broken, too."

"Hmm," I sighed.

We drove by a lone family crypt and Valerie pointed out the window. "Mom, what's that?"

"A crypt the cemetery uses for people waiting to be buried. Grandpa filmed that same crypt over ten years ago for the opening scene of *Dracula*." I referred to the family movies he produced.

"You mean the movie where Dracula comes out of your cedar chest?"

"Yes."

"That movie always scared me."

Mom had been silent since we entered the cemetery. "Will you two stop talking about those movies?"

Lloyd drove slowly to the curb and parked.

"Mom, where's Grandpa's grave?"

"It's right over there." I pointed out the window.

"I don't see it."

Surprised, I gulped. "It's the only grave that has bright green grass on it." The graves we passed and the ones near Dad's were still brown and dry.

Valerie ran ahead of us while Lloyd, Mom and I stepped out of the car. At Dad's grave I looked for an imprint in the grass that the Christmas wreath might have made, but there was none. Perhaps the caretakers had been there.

17

"Look, you can see the casket through this hole in the ground." Valerie pointed at the right side of the grave.

Mom moved near the small opening. "Oh, my God, you can see the vault from here." Unbidden tears streamed down her face. "He didn't want to die. He's not here."

I walked around the grave and stood next to Mom. I bent down and peered into the small gap, wondering where the dirt went. How did the ground at the top of the grave stay up without a foundation?

Lloyd overheard Mom and walked back to the car to see if there was something he could use to cover the opening. When he came back, he held a brick and the plastic cover from the Christmas wreath I'd left in the trunk.

Valerie and I started back toward the car while Lloyd covered the small opening for Mom.

"Mom, what's a vault?" Val asked.

"It's a bigger box the casket is put into to protect us when we die."

"Where's Grandpa? Did he come back?"

Shortly before my father died in the V.A. hospital, he told me he'd "come back" in the spring. When he said this, I thought he meant his health would improve and he'd come home.

I shook my head. "No, Valerie, Grandpa's not coming back."

The office was closed when we left the cemetery. Mom would have to wait until the next day to report the gap in the ground around the vault. We headed for a family restaurant that Mom and Dad always loved. Her eyes looked sad as the hostess showed us to the same table we'd shared the year before. As she ordered a Manhattan, I studied her over my menu. With her flaming red hair and vivacious blue eyes, she could easily have been a stand-in for Lucille Ball. Lucy, too, had married a musician and a vocalist. Cameras, projectors, films, and sound tracks had also played important roles in my parents' lives.

We spoke little at dinner, lost in our own thoughts. Even Valerie was silent. I assumed it was the cemetery experience that affected us. I looked across the table at Mom and couldn't help but think of Dad. All of us missed him terribly, his humor, ingenuity, artistic flair, and golden voice.

18

Dad always told me stories about his life. He learned to play the drums in grade school. Later on he studied under Lee Keller, lead drummer for the Wayne King Orchestra. After that he worked for the Lou Breeze, Will Back, Rudy Austin, and the Glenn Grey Orchestra and performed on radio.

I remembered standing in the kitchen doorway of the two-story house on Octavia Street in Chicago. "Dad, tell me another Army story," I asked.

He looked up from the table. "Let me finish this letter to Pierre. I'll be done in a few minutes."

Fifteen minutes later, Dad came into the living room with a highball in his hand. He sat down on the large blue armchair across from me.

"Did I ever tell you about the time I was stationed at Camp Crowder?"

"I don't think so." I shook my head, disappointed that this story might not be his usual war adventure.

"Let's see, I was stationed in boot camp near Joplin, Missouri, when I met a soldier from Boston. He had a refined speaking voice and a charismatic personality. I started calling him 'Pierre' because of his good looks. We were both in Company B in the 85th Signal Operation Battalion. We shared the same barracks and both of us were teletype operators."

"What's a teletype?"

"It's like a typewriter, but sends out and receives messages by telegraph and prints them when the message is received."

"Oh."

"Anyway, in the spring of 1943, Pierre was working in the office when he overheard the entertainment director looking for someone to represent Camp Crowder at the USO in St. Louis. Pierre told me what he'd done for me when I returned to the barracks after KP duty. He'd spoken to the officer:

'Sir, I couldn't help overhearing that you needed someone to represent the camp. I know of a headliner from Chicago who would be outstanding, Sir.'

'Who do you know, Corporal?'

"Eddie Tillman, Sir. He's on KP duty today, Sir.'

'At ease, Corporal.'

'Thank you, Sir.'

'Is he any good?'

'He's a professional drummer and vocalist. Has a smooth, rich baritone voice. He's been in various orchestras, performed in nightclubs. He's mentioned the Sheraton Hotel in Chicago several times.'

'We only have a week to advertise and put this show together, Corporal. Tell your friend Tillman I want to talk to him'."

Dad smiled. "Well, Diane, when Pierre told me, I just about fell over. I never expected to be called to entertain at the USO, let alone represent the entire camp. The next morning I talked to the entertainment director and found out that my Chicago buddies from the Glenn Grey Orchestra and his "Casalomas" were going to entertain 400 troops from all branches of the service in St. Louis. A week later, on a weekend pass arranged for the boys in Company B, Pierre and I rode the military bus from Camp Crowder to St. Louis. That night, I appeared in front of the largest audience I ever had. Pierre introduced me before each vocal number began."

"Eddie," he'd say, "come down from those drums and give us a song. And now, ladies and gentlemen, the man with the golden voice will sing *When the Lights Go On Again All Over the World*. Later he introduced the song, *I'll Walk Alone* and that night, Diane, I sang the tearjerker, *You'll Never Know*. After that song, they gave me a ten-minute standing ovation. Many tears were shed by both men and women leaving their sweethearts and families for overseas duty. When I tried to sit down at the table reserved in front of the stage, fifteen girls rushed up to me for an autograph."

"Wow! Just like in the movies," I exclaimed. "What about your friend, Pierre?"

"Well, he was a single man. I was married and six years older than him. I took him under my wing. We were like brothers and watched out for each other. Pierre had ten to fifteen girls hugging and kissing him. I remember him telling me during the break his lips were real sore."

"Dad!" I squealed.

Laughing, he leaned over the armrest of the chair for the highball, took a sip and smiled some more.

"Later at the table, Pierre introduced me again, humorously this time, as Errol Flynn's brother."

Dad was dashing and dramatic and he definitely resembled Flynn. I didn't realize how much so until I watched *Captain Blood* and other reruns on the late show. The resemblance was almost uncanny.

❀

"Diane, Diane." Lloyd shook my arm. "What are you thinking about?"

"Nothing." I hesitated, then smiled. "Nothing."

After we drove Mom home from the restaurant, we went to bed early. I fell into a light sleep. Something woke me and I saw my father standing at our bedroom doorway. I squinted in the darkness. He smiled and waved at me. To my surprise, Dad was dressed in the white uniform he had worn daily at the restaurant. I sat up in bed, trying to convince myself that I wasn't dreaming.

I spoke aloud. "You're dead!"

Dad disappeared.

He had looked so happy, waving at me the same way he'd always waved goodnight whenever we backed out of my parents' driveway. On this night, Dad kept his promise to me. He told me he'd come back in the spring, and he did.

❀

After encountering my father's spirit through his favorite music, a spiritual guide entered my life.

CHAPTER THREE:
MY MENTOR

*Find a spiritual mentor who enhances
your spiritual growth*

In early December 1973, I decided to attend a psychic fair, a gathering of people with remarkable talents who give lectures, workshops, and readings of various kinds. I visited a workshop in graphology, the science of reading personalities through handwriting, given by a petite blonde named Barbara Allen. Afterward, she invited me to join a class on self-awareness that started in January 1974.

I felt comfortable when I arrived at Barbara Allen's townhouse, as if I'd known her a long time. She sat for a few moments in a bay window seat to welcome me. When she got up to answer the doorbell, I quickly scanned the room. In the corner to my left stood a four-tier bookcase resting on a large oriental rug. Black and white angel fish swam through a tank leaning against a flight of stairs. A wall mural of colorful, hand-painted butterflies led to the upper rooms.

When the room filled with people, Barbara Allen asked us to share information about ourselves and what we wanted to achieve. Later, she studied a sample of my handwriting for a few moments.

"Diane, you're a writer," she said.

"What, me? Write?" I didn't believe I was good enough in the subjects of English, spelling, and reading.

"Yes! I want you to write something and bring it to class next week."

I always had an inferiority complex about my ability to express myself in this way. Later in life, I realized I had a problem with dyslexia, which meant I unconsciously reversed letters in words while trying to read or write. Ketchup became upketch. The four-digit number 1230 became 1320. At times I lifted words out of sequence from sentences. Unscrambling letters and numbers became a life-long challenge.

All during class that evening, I kept thinking about what I might write, worried that I'd have to stand up in front of the class the following week and recite what I'd written. Hoping for inspiration, I did my best to note what the other students discussed. The next day I decided to write about each person in the class, making a twisted version of what they'd said. Perhaps an *Alice in Wonderland* type of story, giving each student the part of a strange character. After I wrote the story I still didn't feel confident enough to face the class with it.

I got out my tape recorder and a record of odd musical percussion sounds, along with a collection of things to create sound effects—a bell, an alarm clock, a spoon, a glass of water, and a wooden piano bench. I put them all together, changing my voice to fit each character, clanking, clanging, and thumping through my improvisation on the outline I'd prepared.

I felt competent in drama and had helped make many family movies and tapes. All our motion pictures were produced and directed by my father, who infused creativity and entertainment into each holiday. My cousins and I, ages three to eighteen, acted in my father's productions. We called ourselves "The Octavia Players" after the eight of us. One summer, the entire family, including aunts, uncles and grandparents joined the action in an ad-lib, backyard costume satire.

Before filming, Dad interviewed family members using a plastic record-making device. A radio performer and musician, he spoke in a Master of Ceremonies style. Later, he started using a reel-to-reel Webcor recorder, dividing his time between filming and taping. After Dad filmed each holiday group, my cousins and I carried the film box, camera, and lightweight pieces of equipment upstairs to make our homemade production. Mom, aunts, uncles, grandparents stayed downstairs, women to clear the tables and take turns at the sink, while the men talked, laughed and played poker.

After filming, Dad superimposed the title of the story performed by "The Octavia Players" into the film, and edited the scene changes and ending. Film editing and placing the rolls onto a reel were another process in preparing the movie. Music and sound effects were taped and played at each "showing." *The Christmas Carol* and *Murders in the Rue Morgue*, later renamed *The Mad Scientist* for our film, were two of our most memorable tape productions. I acted in the last homemade classic, *Dracula*, at age eighteen.

The following week I brought my new tape to class. The group didn't seem to mind that I'd taped my story because I felt too nervous to read it. To add some suspense, I pushed the play button down slowly. The strange percussion music started, and the class listened, fascinated with each of their stories. They said it sounded good and wanted me to play it again. After we finished the tape, Barbara Allen looked at me.

"And you thought you couldn't write."

I left the tape and gave Barbara Allen permission to use it any way she wanted. Years later, she told me, "You've been in states and cities you don't know about." She played the tape in all her self-awareness classes repeatedly because it demonstrated that people sometimes have to be convinced of their hidden talents.

I also found Barbara Allen's self-awareness classes to be valuable because they taught me a variety of techniques such as self-hypnosis. I learned that hypnosis deals with the mind. How it is used depends upon the instructor, what benefits the student wants to achieve. I enjoyed learning self-hypnosis techniques because they relaxed me. I also became knowledgeable about many other subjects.

I found that many practices I'd considered mind games, such as psychometry—intuitive knowledge of the history of an object—are actually part of the paranormal range of human abilities. Everyone is intuitive. Some can touch an object and visualize a picture of people or places. Still others can go beyond the range of their own faculties into an altered state of mind and become part of the visualization.

Barbara Allen and I had an unusual friendship. We never did what other women friends do, like shopping together or going out for lunch. Instead, we shared our thoughts and ideas.

She was small, blonde, and captivating. I don't believe she ever weighed more than ninety-five pounds. Her looks and her fine, classical clothing drew attention wherever she went. I, on the other hand, possess a sensual look—buxom and fair-complexioned with a reddish cast to my dark hair. Despite our exterior differences we shared the universe in a special way. We totally understood each other, calling each other "sisters of the spirit." I couldn't share my paranormal ability with just anyone; I was afraid people wouldn't understand. But with Barbara Allen, I could be myself. I believe we were destined to meet and learn from each other.

If you were to ask me to name only one thing I'd give Barbara Allen credit for, it would be her help redirecting my gifts in a positive manner. She also introduced me to advanced hypnotic relaxation techniques, past life regression, the use of colored candles in ritual, as well as psychometry visualization and the study of the body's energy centers, called chakras.

During one of the advanced classes that Barbara Allen held in her living room, she taught about different colors of candles and how we could use them in prayer and meditation. She lowered the lights and drew our attention to a number of candles she'd placed around the room.

"The green candle is for health and it's also for wealth," she told us, walking over to a small table and lifting a green candle for us to see. "If someone is sick, light a green candle for them." She demonstrated for us. "The yellow candle is for fertility and intelligence." As she spoke she lit each one and held it up.

I sat comfortably, listening and watching her, noting aspects of her appearance. She wore short brown suede boots, worn slightly at the toes. A black skirt hugged her tiny hips and an old-fashioned cameo graced the closed collar of her full- sleeved beige blouse. As she moved around the room, I wondered, is she a witch? What in the world had I gotten myself into? And what will I ever do with the knowledge of candle colors?

As I was thinking, I focused on Barbara Allen. She turned to me, her long blonde hair moving with the motion of her body.

"Diane, you wanted to say something?"

We smiled at one another, but I stammered a little, feeling as if I'd been caught in some mischief.

"Uh, what is the blue candle for?"

There was a slight smile on her face as she lit the blue candle and picked it up. "Blue, Diane, is the color of oceans and the universe. It's a psychic color, calm yet powerful."

A decade passed before I put into motion what I learned in Barbara Allen's class.

One afternoon, ten years after Barbara Allen explained the significance of the color blue, my daughter Valerie phoned me.

"Mom, something's happening in this apartment," she said, her voice tense. "When I get my set of keys, they aren't where I put them. And you know how I always keep my hairbrush in the bathroom? Well, when I got home from work today, it was in the plant in the living room. Could you come over and check things out? Feel for vibrations that don't belong here?"

At the time, Valerie had not expressed much interest in spirituality. She knew I had some knowledge of metaphysics because of my classes with Barbara Allen. Before I went to Val's apartment, I was able to reassure her that I'd learned how to rid a house of unwanted energies through prayer or with metaphysical methods, such as lighting a candle.

When I arrived at Valerie's apartment, we started to chat, but she stopped in mid-sentence. "Mom, there are little lights around your head."

"There are?" I was surprised that Valerie could see the lights. I laughed a little, trying to keep her calm. "Okay, let's not get carried away." Valerie often overreacted to paranormal experiences because of her lack of knowledge.

"Can you start now?" she asked, meaning could I put myself into a meditative state.

Methodically relaxing my body and closing my eyes, I spoke softly, telling her what I sensed. "I see a thin, dark-haired girl. Her hair is long. I feel she's a gentle person."

When I opened my eyes, Valerie said, "I knew it. I knew someone was here."

"Valerie, she's a sensitive person. Just tell the spirit to leave you alone."

The next evening, Valerie telephoned me again. She sounded hysterical. She told me she'd called a paranormal investigator. Whatever he'd told her had frightened her. However, he said that for a price he'd get rid of the presence haunting her apartment. I decided I'd better visit again. This time I armed myself with a blue candle. I remembered what Barbara Allen had said about blue, the calm, powerful and psychic color of the universe.

When I entered Valerie's apartment, words rushed out of her in a torrent. "Mom, I don't know what you're going to think of all this. Yesterday I saw a reflection of the girl's spirit on the blank screen of my television." She also saw the spirit looking out the large picture window in the living room. "And before you got here, the volume indicator on my stereo moved ten notches higher by itself!"

I told Valerie that I hadn't used a candle in ten years. After I unwrapped the blue candle from the tissue paper, I lit it. I calmly asked Valerie to watch me from the kitchen. I held the candle, walked into the living room, closed my eyes and silently asked the gentle spirit to leave. *My daughter doesn't understand why you're here*, I told her. *Your presence frightens her. Please leave.*

A few moments passed. I opened my eyes. I think Valerie expected more.

"Is that all?" she asked, walking into the living room.

I nodded yes. "She's gone. I saw her leave through the back door."

I stayed a few minutes longer, and Valerie's eyes were calm when she thanked me for coming over. "Call me if you have any more trouble, honey," I said, kissing her cheek.

Driving home, I wondered where my continued interest in the supernatural was leading me. What purpose did it have in my life? My mind flashed on Barbara Allen. "Remember," she'd once said, "there will come a day when the student becomes the teacher. Perhaps that time will come sooner than you realize."

Although I didn't know it then, the time fast approached when my spiritual mentor's words would prove prophetically true.

CHAPTER FOUR:
THE AWAKENING

Protect yourself from the thoughts of others

As the years passed after my father's death, I worked at my mother's restaurant as a fill-in for every job from cook and dishwasher to waitress and bookkeeper. At the same time, I joined a community theater group and gained experience in character acting. I took college courses in psychology and science. The following year, Barbara Allen continued to coach me via cassette tapes in the metaphysical arts, heightening my understanding of theology, numerology, astrology and Eastern philosophy.

Soon I had enough knowledge of the metaphysical arts to begin giving lectures on numerology for ladies' groups. I also started compiling astrological charts for people. During this period, each of these interests became my hobbies and helped satisfy my deep desire to know and understand myself. I'd always had a deep affection for astrology, but now friends and neighbors asked me to compile their charts so they could gain better insight into their lives.

One day I visited the drugstore near our home. My pharmacist waited on me as usual and rang up my purchase. As he operated the cash register, I noticed his eyes filling with pain. Looking at him made me hurt, too.

"What's the matter, Sam?"

"I have this terrible headache," he told me.

"There's a doctor right next door," I reminded him.

"Yes, but he's not my doctor," he said, rubbing the back of his neck.

I wanted to do something to help take his mind off the pain, so I asked him for his birth date. He knew I gave some of his employees astrological readings and he took my receipt, turned it over, and wrote his birth date on it. When he handed it back to me, I cupped my hands over his as a gesture of sympathy.

"Well, I'd better go, Sam. I'll start on your chart. Call your doctor. Maybe he can give you some help. Hope you feel better soon."

He looked directly at me, the pain still vibrating from his eyes. "Thanks, Diane."

At home, I sat down at the portable typewriter on my desk, typed his name and birth date across the top of a piece of white paper, and began the process of outlining his chart. Later I'd return to the drugstore and offer it as a gift to help Sam feel better. I felt fine until I neared the halfway point and my hands began trembling. I rubbed them together, then leaned over my work and started again. My hands trembled and started to cramp. I couldn't finish his chart. Frustrated, I yanked the paper from the machine, crumpled it into a ball and threw it into the wastebasket. Preparing a chart had never affected me physically before. Certainly, my hands never trembled while doing one. Two days later a neighbor told me that my pharmacist had died of a cerebral hemorrhage. It was then I realized I'd tapped into his energy field when I touched his hands in the drugstore. My reaction was caused from the combination of gathering information about my pharmacist by physically touching him and focusing on his birth chart.

My interest in astrology lasted many years, but with one difference. I never again tried to complete a full chart. The experience with my pharmacist showed me I pick up on more than I bargain for. Without the knowledge to control these reactions, preparing astrological charts and doing other metaphysical work for others might complicate my life.

At this point, I decided to combine my interest in astrological sun signs with numerology. When asked about these interests, I lumped all my different hobbies into one and simply told people "astrology." If I mentioned my other interests, such as psychometry, hypnosis techniques, or numerology, people might have thought I was involved in the occult and that just wasn't true. I used a combination of sun signs, numerology, and my intuitive abilities to help people understand themselves and improve their lives. By coaching others, I began to realize my own spiritual gifts.

While I learned more about metaphysical methods of self-discovery, I had a lesson to learn about protecting myself from negative energy fields. The problem hadn't occurred to me until I experienced an unforgettable psychic reaction. One evening I used a combination of numerology and psychometry in a demonstration at a women's group. After the meeting, an excruciating pain gripped my head when I went to bed. Since I'd lectured on numerology earlier that evening, I decided to use another metaphysical method to release the pressure.

Over a decade had passed since Barbara Allen briefly touched upon the subject of chakras, the energy centers of the body, in one of her self-awareness classes. What I remembered of her discussion focused upon the psychic center of the body located at the crown of the head, a chakra point she referred to as the "lotus."

I visualized a lotus flower at the top of my head. As it opened, it released a powerful flow of energy moving with great speed and force. To release the negative energy, I visualized it dispersing from my crown chakra. I felt the energy dissipate, leaving me free of pain.

I realized it wasn't the use of astrology or numerology that caused the headache, but my own touch. If I used psychometry in conjunction with people rather than items, it caused adverse reactions in me. Just as important, I noticed my vulnerability to all sorts of psychic disorders and illnesses over the years by not protecting myself from other people's energy fields.

I continued helping others gain insight by using my interests separately. This protected me from negative psychic reactions. Later, I realized psychometry's many beneficial applications. It's used by police departments around the world to solve crimes. But I discovered a more practical, humane purpose. Psychometry can be used to pinpoint illnesses in others through touch.

In the following years, I learned to protect myself. I don't pretend to know everything about psychic attacks but I've learned a great deal from my own experiences. Sometimes people with problems bombard others with negative thoughts. This type of behavior is called a psychic attack. These assaults are of a belittling nature, meant to lower your self-esteem and destroy any effort at elevating yourself to a higher spiritual level.

Many of these intrusions, I believe, are caused by unresolved conflicts within the attacker. If you look at the nature of the assault, you can analyze where the attacker's anxiety lies. When you see someone is using you to buffer their own emotional pain, there's something you can do about their behavior: don't respond. In this way, you can remain understanding and powerful and maintain your level of spirituality. This "no response" method can be difficult. As you recall others' insults and the repressed anger you feel, you could easily respond at the attackers' level and suffer from your own hostile attitude.

The attacker may be unconscious of the issues driving his feelings. To protect himself from pain, he tries passing his unhappiness to you. When you're attacked often, perhaps three or four times a week and are affected by it, you may become spiritually sick from the overload. If you continue to stay on overload, you may suffer anxiety and the illnesses connected with it. The hurt you endure as you relive the abuse in memories and dreams is beyond the normal range of suffering. It's this depth of pain that causes people to stay at lower levels of spirituality. Remove yourself from the company of those whose words hurt you, so you don't give up your spiritual goals.

Psychic attacks depend on vulnerabilities. The attacker gambles on using the weak and receptive. If he or she fails to disempower you, others will be enlisted to join in the pursuit to control you. Don't be afraid; the truth of his intentions will eventually come out. During psychologically painful times, reciting the Lord's Prayer or the Twenty-third Psalm to maintain spiritual stamina makes a difference. Others use the combination of prayer and visualization.

While you pray, bathe yourself in the white light of God. Encircle yourself with His light in a protective cocoon. Picture the Lord's expression as He holds your face between His hands. The calming effect releases your spirit from overload. Attacks glance off the armor of the cocoon you've created by immersing yourself in prayer and visualization. With this method you cannot be affected by the negative thoughts and plans of others.

When you place yourself in the Lord's care, sometimes a glow of loving-kindness brightens your eyes and face and could be mistaken for a beautiful complexion. The late Pope John Paul II and the Dalai Lama are two world-renowned figures known for this glow.

Learning to protect myself while helping others became a crucial factor in my goal of fulfilling the spiritual purpose Christ intended for me.

Soon my daughter Valerie and my mother would teach me about the value of dream interpretation, an important lesson in my spiritual development.

CHAPTER FIVE: PORTALS OF DREAMS

Find awareness in your dreams

Eight years had passed. Valerie was now seventeen. Curly-headed and energetic, she'd inherited the golden voice that runs in the family. Lloyd and I were proud of Valerie and her clear, smooth voice; at times she accompanied herself on the guitar and we loved to hear her sing.

One night in May of 1981, we heard Valerie yelling to us from her bedroom. I leaped out of bed and rushed to her room. Though in bed, she couldn't move. I sat down next to her and rubbed her arms and legs until she relaxed.

"You're all right, Val. You're all right," I said. "You've been dreaming."

In the morning she seemed fine, as if nothing unusual had occurred. The next night it happened again. Lloyd and I rushed to her side. This time, she lay in a fetal position in her bed, unable to move or talk; her mouth was closed and her jaw clenched.

"Move your legs, Valerie," I urged her. After a few moments she relaxed enough to go back to sleep. Lloyd and I walked out of her room, feeling frightened.

"Lloyd," I whispered when we got back to our room, "do you think she's on drugs?"

"I don't know," he replied evenly. Lloyd is calm under pressure. He was worried too, but didn't show it.

"If this happens again, we'd better take her to the doctor." We climbed back into bed.

The next night Valerie yelled again. This time, when I entered her room, she was on her stomach.

"Valerie, you're all right," I assured her. Her physical reaction didn't last as long as it had before.

In the morning, I went to check on her. She was already up, listening to her records. She looked perfectly fine.

"Val, tell me about it. What's happening?" I fully expected her to tell me that she was on drugs and I hoped I'd know how to handle the news. I certainly didn't expect her to start telling me about a dream.

"Well, I'm in a plane over water, and I'm parachuting out. I jump out of the plane and tug on the cord, but my parachute won't open. I hit the water so hard I can't move. Mom, it felt like I was hitting cement. It physically hurt. When I had the dream last night, I went down into the water and saw this big ugly fish. I hit the water the same way. In the dreams I can't move or talk."

I thought for a moment. "I never really studied dream interpretation, but you mention a fish. There's an astrological sign of the fish for birthdates between February 20 and March 20. The only fish I know is your grandmother. She's a Pisces."

At the time, I hadn't paid much attention to dreams. Relieved, I just dismissed it. Valerie appeared to forget about it, too.

A week later, I picked up my mother at her beauty parlor. On the way back to her house, she told me she didn't feel well.

"Do you want to go to the doctor? I can drive you there now."

"No, he'll just give me too much medicine and I'll take it, then I'll be sick all weekend," she said in a weak voice. "I have too much to do."

When we arrived at her house, I helped her put a few things away. As we worked I said, "Mom, as soon as we finish here, get into bed."

Rather than answering me, she reached into her breadbox and handed me a large, uniquely shaped cookie.

"What's this?" I asked as I took it from her.

"It's called an elephant ear cookie." The shape did resemble an elephant ear. "Maybe it'll bring you luck."

"Either that, or I'll be hearing some really big news!"

As I walked out the back door to get into my car, I said, "I'll pick you up for dinner on Monday, Mom. Thanks for the elephant ear." We smiled and waved goodnight.

I don't know what made me call Mom on Sunday. At two in the afternoon I dialed her number, but there wasn't an answer. Finally, as night fell, I called family members and friends who might have taken her out. No one had seen her. Sensing something wrong, Lloyd and I drove to her house. By now it was eight in the evening.

The house was completely dark when we pulled into her driveway. First we checked her front and back entryways. The screen doors were hooked from the inside. Lloyd broke through the screen of the back door and unhooked it, then opened the back door with my key. He turned on several lights as we walked through the house. We found Mom lying on her stomach on the ocean blue carpeting of her living room.

Kneeling, I spoke to her. "Mom? Mom, Lloyd and I are here."

She lifted her head, unable to talk. Her eyes were open, staring straight ahead without expression. With my heart pounding, I looked up at Lloyd. "Do you think she's had a stroke?"

"I don't know but I think we'd better call the paramedics." He walked to the telephone.

I touched Mom's swollen right hand and gingerly lifted each of her fingers, which felt stiff. All these years she'd worked so hard, only to have a stroke. As I looked up, the Italian mermaid chandelier that hung over her small living room table caught my eye. Then I remembered Valerie's dream! It didn't have the same setting, but her dream had all the elements of this scene.

Mom had always been intuitive yet she was never interested in science or the paranormal. She could perceive something immediately without any special information. Years before her stroke, she warned me about a girlfriend of mine. "Watch that one; she'll cause you problems," she'd said.

"Oh, you're wrong," I replied. "She's not like that. She wouldn't cause me any trouble. I don't believe it."

My friend had come from an abusive and unstable family. She had learned from her father how to humiliate people deliberately, an abuse I witnessed on numerous occasions. As we grew older, I noticed that she had developed what seemed like a mean streak. Throughout the many years of our friendship, I thought if I could show her true caring, she'd change. It didn't work. She loved to hurt me and seemed to enjoy attacking me. She turned other friends against me, and I began to feel everything was my fault.

My girlfriend did indeed cause me problems, as my mother had warned me years before. After I severed ties with her, I still heard that she remains unhappy, ungrateful, and rude. I no longer consider her my friend.

I remember one of Mom's prophetic dreams. I had been in the living room trying to finish a high school World History report on tools and weapons used by primitive people. Mom called, "Diane, would you come here a minute?" When I entered her bedroom, Mom sat at her French provincial vanity, delicately applying auburn pencil strokes to her light eyebrows. "I want to tell you about a dream I had last night."

"Oh, is that all," I answered, uninterested.

"Since you're working on a report about primitive and ancient people, Diane, I think you'll find it interesting."

I leaned against the wall and waited for her to continue.

She turned to face me, rose from the vanity and said, "I dreamed of lying in an Egyptian casket."

"Were you dead?"

"Well, of course I was dead!" Noticing the smile on my face, she said, "You're just like your father, always making jokes. I'm serious, Diane. Do you want to hear this dream or not?"

When I nodded, she continued relating her dream.

"I was in an Egyptian casket with my arms folded across my chest, holding an Egyptian scepter in each hand. I was dressed in white and gold. I noticed a lot of gold around me, and a stone of black onyx was in the casket with me. She folded her arms across her breasts to demonstrate and I noticed her Indian arrowhead necklace, a gift from her father, lying against her chest.

"Mom, that Indian arrowhead you're wearing, well, I've read that primitive people used obsidian, and you called the stone in the casket black onyx. Could it have been obsidian? Was it black and shiny? Or was it glassy like your arrowhead?"

She stepped into her skirt, pulled it up over her hips and turned to zip and button it. "Come to think of it, Diane, the stone did have more of a glassy look."

"Where was it in the casket?"

"On top of me, I think. No, it was beneath my crossed arms." A little smile flitted across her face. "Perhaps, a long time ago in another time, I was a queen."

That dream fits you, I thought. You're dominating, driving, beautiful, and wear the most fashionable clothing from the finest stores. Grandma had even called the other day and asked how "Queenie" was doing.

"Maybe there's something to the dream, Diane. It was so vivid."

"When I'm in the library tomorrow, I'll try to find something on Egypt or mummies for you." The next day after school I handed her three library books on ancient Egypt. Later that evening she called me into her bedroom.

"I didn't find much that seems related to the dream, but one book did have something about the Egyptian heart scarab."

Opening the book, she began to read. "The heart scarab amulet came into use during the First Intermediate period. It was traditionally made out of obsidian." Mom glanced up at me, then continued reading. "An important amulet, it was to be included in the mummy wrappings with close proximity to the heart." [1]

"Wow! Is that neat! Is that ever cool! What do you think the dream means now?"

"I'm not sure. I guess we'll just have to think about it a little more."

At the time, I felt she was hiding something connected with the dream. Within a year, at the height of my parents' business success, Mom was diagnosed with an enlarged heart and a damaged valve caused by a bout with rheumatic fever when she was twenty-one. After finding out she had these conditions she always wore the obsidian necklace and never mentioned the dream again.

---

[1] El Mahdy, Christine. *Mummies, Myth and Magic.* New York: Thames and Hudson, 1989.

During the 1980s, Valerie began having premonition dreams. The ability was natural for the women in our family and no one worked at developing it. Nobody even talked about it openly except for my mother's sister, Aunt Luana.

Many years ago, when my cousin Rita and I were five and six, respectively, Rita's mother, Aunt Luana, dreamed of dying in an auto accident.

I remember standing in Grandma Verda's kitchen watching her and my step-grandfather Harry, Aunt Luana, Uncle Dick and Rita as they planned a Sunday drive to Naperville, a town a few miles away. I felt a bit hurt and rejected I couldn't go along because there wasn't enough room in the car.

Aunt Luana's voice was almost defiant when she interrupted the discussion. "I don't want to go. I dreamed last night that I'd be killed in a car accident." She pulled her beautiful face into a death mask.

"Oh, Lu, it's just a dream. Nothing's going to happen." For the longest time, all of them stood in the kitchen talking at once.

My parents, who lived upstairs in my grandmother's two-story house, came downstairs to chat with them for a few minutes. My father realized that I wanted to go with my relatives but knew what little room there was in their car. "Go on ahead. Diane is going to Starved Rock with us today."

I'd never heard that name before and I didn't know Starved Rock was a state park. I still wanted to go with Rita.

Uncle Dick picked Rita up in his arms. "Let's go," he said, imitating The Great Gildersleeve, a favorite radio comedian. One by one, they trailed out of the house.

"Bye, be careful and have a good time," my parents called from the door.

"Have a good time yourself," they replied, smiling and waving as they strode to the car.

The house was quiet again. My parents went back upstairs, and I stood at Grandma's living room window, watching my relatives get into the little Ford coupe. Uncle Dick ushered Rita into the back seat to sit between my grandparents. Aunt Luana, who usually smiled often, still appeared apprehensive as she climbed into the front seat.

I watched the car go down the street, until it turned the corner and disappeared.

It was late in the evening when we returned from Starved Rock. As we got out of our car and neared the house, I could hear our upstairs telephone ringing. My mother turned the key in the door, and I pushed it open and ran up the stairs to answer it.

"Hello?" I said.

"Hello, Mrs. Donna Tillman, this is Aurora calling . . . Aurora calling," the operator repeated.

My mother entered the room. "They want you, Mommie." I held out the receiver. As my father came into the room I stepped back, sensing this was an important call. He and I stood side-by-side, facing her. There was pain in my mother's eyes as she listened to the voice at the other end of the line, and her face turned white with fear.

"They were in an auto accident . . . it was critical. They're in the hospital in Aurora . . . all five were hurt!"

It wasn't until the next morning that I heard what had happened. During the afternoon they'd stopped at an apple orchard, and on the way back to my grandmother's home, the accident had occurred. Grandma Verda received facial injuries and both legs were broken. My Grandfather Harry had a broken leg and head injuries. Uncle Dick, who was driving the car, suffered a crushed liver and a broken leg. My cousin lost one of her eyes and also suffered a broken leg. Rita's mother, Aunt Luana, who was riding in the passenger seat, hit the rearview mirror as she flew out the windshield, causing severe head injuries. She died in the accident, just as she had predicted.

These experiences showed me how important dreams are to spiritual awareness. But I still needed to learn about dealing with the dangers of psychic phenomena. Christ would help me find the positive balance between the physical and the metaphysical worlds.

Chapter Six:
Conquering Evil

Christ's teachings keep evil away

When Valerie was a teenager, she often brought books home from the library about the paranormal and disappeared into her bedroom for most of the evening.

One afternoon, with Valerie at the library and Mom taking her daily nap, I left the house to run a few errands. When I returned, I heard muffled whispering at the back door landing. At first I thought there'd been a power failure while I was out, and the radio had come on automatically when the power was restored. As I walked through the house, I looked in on Mom. She was still napping.

That night Valerie called me to her bedroom. "Mom," she said, "something's tugging at my toes while I'm in bed."

"Oh, it's probably a muscle spasm, Val."

"Mom, I don't think so. I think there's something in my room."

"You mean a poltergeist is playing with your toes? Come on, Val," I said, half-laughing. "Ever since we took that Halloween bus tour of haunted cemeteries, you've thought we brought home a poltergeist from the Scottish lounge where we stopped. He's gone, Val. Spirits go back where they feel comfortable. Now go to sleep and stop thinking about this silliness."

I didn't mention the whispering I'd been hearing for weeks at the back door entrance. Or mention she needed to stop reading her paranormal books for awhile. Why upset her? I thought. Besides, I couldn't be sure of a connection between the eerie sounds and Valerie's feeling that something was in her room.

That night, Lloyd came home from work just after midnight. I always waited up for him; it was our time alone together. About an hour later we went to bed.

I started dreaming about a little man who sexually harassed me. Dressed in a black hat and cape, he had an extremely large nose and a bumpy complexion. He stood on Lloyd's side of the bed, looking directly at me. I knew telepathically what he wanted. I stood on my side of the bed, directly facing this grotesque being.

I took my large cross from the dresser and placed it in front of my torso. The little fellow became angry at my gesture. He flashed a sinister smile and watched me closely, waiting for my reaction as he attempted to lift Lloyd's arm. I rebuked him, holding the cross out at arm's length, and ordered his evil spirit to leave my home. He disappeared.

When I opened my eyes, the bedside clock read 3:00 a.m. I felt a little shaken, but I got up and went into the kitchen to write a short note to Valerie:

> Dear Val,
> You were right. There was something in the house. Don't worry. I took care of it. That evil spirit knows I'm not afraid of him, and Christ dwells within.
>
> Love, Mom

A couple of hours later Valerie stood over me, shaking my shoulder. Wake up, wake up, Mom," she whispered. "I'm afraid to be alone. I want to talk."

"Mm, uh, okay," I mumbled, drowsy. In a few moments I crawled out of bed, grumbling to myself, wondering if I'd ever get any sleep. I made my way into the kitchen and sat at the table. Valerie, who had just finished washing her hair at this early hour, stood by the kitchen sink with her back toward me. As she wrapped the towel around her head, she turned and noticed me sitting there.

"Mom, what do you mean about the evil spirit, not to worry, I took care of it?" She pointed to the note on the table.

"I related my dream to her. You were right, Val."

"Oh, my God," she said. "I'm reading a book from the library about an evil spirit that sexually attacks people through their subconscious while they sleep. You described him almost word-for-word."

I looked at her solemnly. "Valerie, please don't bring home any more books about evil spirits, poltergeists, or black magic. What you don't realize is that half the people in the world have evil spirits in their homes. Even if they were aware of it, they wouldn't have any idea how they got in. Why do you think there's so much madness in the world?"

When people ignore higher consciousness and choose a lower path, they attract evil spirits or entities. Sometimes we attract these entities into our homes for other reasons. Searching for a spiritual path can also make us susceptible to attacks from lower forces. Attacks may become more frequent as we reach higher levels of spirituality. Christ allows us to work out our own problems. The more we search for Christ and pray, the better we are at keeping evil at bay.

"Val," I continued, "I have a clean house. There's no reason for interference from evil spirits. I know you've noticed my candles burning on the stove. Did you think I put them there only because they're pretty? I light them and pray to Christ every day to help my mother and to protect us."

"But, Mom," Val interrupted, "why did it come to us? We're good people."

"I've read that we create our own evil with anger and other negative thoughts and emotions, and then it attacks us."

"Is it because we're having a hard time with Grandma living here?"

"Perhaps. Or you brought it home from the library in that book."

"Mom, that sounds silly. What do you mean, in that book?"

"Well, Val, all things have an energy vibrating around them. I talk to our houseplants, and the flowers in the yard, and I talk to the trees. I tell them how beautiful they are, touch them, stroke them, and truly love them. My love vibration enters them by thoughts and touch. We can also receive positive or negative information through the energy transferred from people and objects without realizing it. You and other people touched and read the book. The only difference between that book and my plants is the book's negative vibrations. Its energy was strong enough to enter our home."

"You mean anything I touch gets my thoughts?" Val wrinkled her brow.

"Yes, and most people wouldn't know how to get rid of the negativity," I answered firmly.

After a few moments I said, "Val, since I'm up now, I think I'll make a cup of tea. It's been a long morning."

"Stay in the kitchen, Mom. Please? I'll get my makeup and come back." She hurried off to her room.

I got up from the table and proceeded to make a cup of tea. Glancing at the kitchen clock, I noticed it was 6:15 a.m. "What a morning," I said to myself.

Val came back into the kitchen with her blouse in one hand and a hairbrush and makeup bag in another. "Oh, you decided to stay up. Thanks, Mom."

I nodded and cautiously sipped the steaming tea. "Boy, that's hot." I set the cup down on the saucer. "Do you know the word psychometry? The study of psychometry explains vibrations, the power of touch and thought." I smiled at her. "Remember how you made me hold Dad's and my gift while it was still wrapped last Christmas? As I held it, I told you I saw a candle on a table, dinner for two, and heard music."

"Yes, you knew what it was. No more holiday gifts for you, Mom!" she joked.

"I didn't know you had given me two tickets for *The Music Man* at the Candlelight Dinner playhouse. But my senses picked up an image of the evening you intended for us when I held the package."

Vibrations, touch, and thought . . . "That was a good vibration. You bought the gift with love and brought it into this house with good intention."

"Well, what about evil vibrations?" Val asked.

"Same way, but the attitudes are negative—like greed, anger, jealousy, and hate."

Val started applying her makeup as I looked across the table at her.

I took another sip of tea. "A good example of the evil that may come into a home is the negative energy created when two people go through a particularly difficult divorce. Take your Aunt Genny's life, for instance. Her first husband's drinking made it worse. She had problems with your little cousins, financial difficulties, and lived in constant fear. It was heartbreaking to watch. And even though the divorce was a very bad time for her, she tried living under the same roof with her ex-husband afterward. She went to church every week to pray and talk to the priest. Ten years passed and nothing seemed to help. Nothing made the situation better because all that had been done, said, touched, or thought remained in their house. Finally, Aunt Genny took her children, a few belongings, and moved to another town. But the difficulties didn't stop, because after a few months her children went back into their father's home. They returned to a totally alcoholic and broken environment where they were always in trouble. The father's personality plus the evil spirit that his ill will brought in created evil from the negative vibrations.

Valerie was brushing her hair and stopped with the hairbrush in mid-air. "Why isn't it like that for Aunt Genny anymore?"

"When she met and married Bobby, he turned her life around. Bobby's very spiritual and kind-hearted and he loves Aunt Genny very much. I know he prays and buys roses for the Virgin of Guadalupe and he lights a white candle to her. He told me once that he prays for everyone he loves. Val, he prays for your father, you, and me. I guess you might say he found the power of prayer by praying for others. Only sweet sounds come out of Bobby's mouth. Love and good vibrations fill their home."

Valerie quietly absorbed all I'd said.

I thought of another aspect of prayer. "Did I ever tell you how the Virgin of Guadalupe helped Grandma Verda after the accident?"

"I don't remember you mentioning it."

Images of events after that fatal car accident flooded my mind. Grandma Verda was the last one to return home from the hospital. After all these years, I still recall the large red and cream-colored ambulance parked in front of the two-story house. The attendants carried Grandma Verda into her converted dining room and lay her on a hospital bed, her body covered in a hard, white full body cast.

"My father made arrangements for my mother to stay home from the restaurant to take care of Grandma Verda. My grandmother's brothers, sister, and their spouses filled in for various jobs and helped my parents keep the family businesses in operation. My mother bathed Grandma, styled her henna colored hair and cooked all her meals. Grandma healed slowly and she cried often."

"After a year, Grandma Verda's body cast was removed, her once beautiful legs were left stick-like and unbending. She sat in her wheelchair, saddened and pale. Her recovery would be a long and difficult journey; she knew it and so did we."

"What happened next?" Valerie always wanted to surge ahead.

"Now wait a minute, I'm trying to build a picture for you. Here's where the power of prayer comes in. In 1952, my step-grandfather Harry made handrails for Grandma so she could relearn to walk. At night, when Harry came home from work he'd help her practice. Her attempts to walk were painful and we saw little improvement. In the meantime, Will and Mary, Dad's cousins, pressed Mom and Dad to join them for a vacation in Mexico. Their first stop would be the shrine of the Virgin of Guadalupe in Mexico City. My parents left Grandma in the care of her sister, my aunt Dot, and their relatives. About two weeks after Mom and Dad left, I found a picture postcard on the stairs leading to our apartment. The photo showed the shrine's interior, where hundreds of crutches and braces belonging to people miraculously healed lay in front of the altar. The postcard read that the four of them had prayed at the shrine of the Virgin of Guadalupe for Grandma Verda."

Valerie smiled and nodded. "Oh, I know what happened."

I smiled back, recalling that mystical month. "A little over a week after Mom and Dad left for Mexico, Grandma Verda shuffled through the house, down the outside stairs, and onto the sidewalk holding Harry's arm. Her legs wouldn't bend and she wasn't physically perfect, but she could walk. Three weeks later, Mom and Dad returned home, unaware a miracle had happened until Grandma Verda stood at the front door and welcomed their arrival."

"Wow," Valerie said, amazed.

"For years, Grandma Verda had been the matriarch and the foundation of her family. Heaven touched Grandma and allowed her to be a leader again. The color had returned to her cheeks. She was able to play the piano, sew, garden, wash clothes, and cook dinner. Mom got Grandma interested in having holiday parties, painting by numbers, shell jewelry making and crocheting. Grams made a black, green and fuchsia throw for her."

"One evening at a wedding reception, Harry helped her stand and put her crutch aside. As he tightly held her, she rested her feet on his shoes and they began to dance. It seemed like years since I'd heard her laugh or saw her smile"....Yes, and the entire family still feels grateful to the Virgin of Guadalupe for interceding on Grandma's behalf. It's important you remember the power of prayer and how it can turn lives around."

Val rose from the table and slipped into her blouse. "Thanks, Mom, for staying up and explaining all of this." She glanced at the clock on the kitchen wall. "I'd better get going... I want to stop at the library and return that book before I go to work."

"Good girl! Valerie, someday you may have to attack evil for yourself or for me. Your faith in God will save you. You're going to learn there's only one way to attack it; don't be afraid. Tell it to leave! Remember that Jesus said 'Get thee hence, Satan' when the demon was tempting Him.[2] Rebuke evil in the name of Jesus Christ, for with Him, all things are possible. The key is to resist the devil in your mind and he will leave you... do me a favor, Val. Don't put the book in the front seat of the car while you're driving. Wrap it up in an old towel and put it in the trunk."

"Okay, Mom, I understand. You don't have to explain that one!"

---

[2] Matthew 4:10, King James version: "Get thee hence, Satan, for it is written thou shalt worship the Lord thy God, and him only shalt thou serve."

Through prayer, I realized I could help others and fulfill the mission Christ gave me. I knew God was at my side giving me strength and courage as I prayed. Next, I needed to learn how to accept the help of heavenly visitors.

Chapter Seven: Heaven Is On My Side

Accept help from heavenly visitors

Through the years I'd often heard my father's music, the words of his songs, popping into my head at random. One day, when I stood in the kitchen sorting canna flower bulbs that Mom had prepared before her illness, I heard Dad's music again. I closed my eyes to listen and became aware of his spirit standing in front of me. He looked the same in life except his shirt was the whitest white I've ever seen; his skin glowed and his face was without a blemish. He said all the plans he and Mom made weren't going to manifest and if I needed help, he would be there.

There was no question in my mind I'd heard Dad communicate, but I questioned my own senses. I needed to prove to myself that his words weren't simply my imagination. And for the first time since I'd started having visitations from Heaven, I began asking questions.

Dad, what's Heaven like?

It's beautiful, Diane, he related telepathically. *I'm in another dimension, but there are mountains, grass, and flowers. I see all our relatives who left earth before I did. We have music all the time.*

I smiled at the thought of the family parties they must be enjoying. I pulled out a chair and sat at the kitchen table. Dad's spirit sat across from me. He said Lloyd and I should go out more often and told me our lives would be different from his and Mom's. He'd support me while we took care of Mom and I closed the restaurant, explaining

53

I didn't realize how much love surrounded me. Proud all our relatives knew of my spiritual work and its purpose, he said someday others would know of me, too.

I told him telepathically I felt safe and knew I wasn't alone. At that moment Mom walked into the kitchen, sat down at the table, and pulled her gold cigarette case from the pocket of her robe. As she tapped her cigarette lightly on the case, I said to her, "Mom, Dad's here." I pointed to the empty chair across from me. "He's sitting right there."

Mom looked at me, cigarette poised in mid-air. Her face said it all. Most people would have the same reaction: Poor thing. It's been too much for Diane these past few years, selling her mom's house, closing the restaurant, working with the doctors and lawyers, and running off to college three days a week for classes. She's having some type of breakdown.

I started laughing and turned to the empty chair. *Sorry, Dad, she doesn't believe it.* He knew she wouldn't and he smiled.

Contacts with Dad became more frequent as we continued caring for Mom in our home. Dad was there for me while he waited for Mom to join him. My burdens weren't as heavy as others thought because Heaven allowed my father's spirit to be with us. Even though it was stressful to watch my mother's physical condition deteriorate, I accepted God's plan for her.

One morning I walked into Mom's bedroom to prepare her for the day. I gave her a sponge bath, an insulin injection, and emptied the catheter, everything a licensed practical nurse would have done.

"Good morning, Mom," I said. Her smile greeted me in return. I unwrapped the gauze around her toes. The tissue there was beginning to deteriorate, and this morning her toes had a purplish cast just under the skin. I recognized it as the onset of skin ulcers.

"Oh, Mom." For the first time in seven years, tears welled up in my eyes and rolled down my cheeks. "I can't save your feet. I tried, but I can't save them."

She grabbed my hand. Not wanting her to see my heartache, I turned and left the room. My mother had been an excellent dancer as a young girl, and now her legs were failing her. Mom's knees were drawn up in a bent position, contracted, the visiting nurse said, and her condition had recently grown worse.

I went into the kitchen. "God knows what He's doing," I repeated over and over. My heart ached, yet I knew that Heaven was on my side. I blotted tears from my eyes and started washing the dishes. After a few minutes, I went back to Mom's bedroom, powdered her skin, and helped her into a fresh nightgown. As I worked on her, the scent of roses encircled me. Twenty-four years earlier, Grandma had signaled her presence with the fragrance of roses.

I spoke telepathically: *Grandma Verda, is that you? Are you the angel of roses? You have every right to watch me now. We all watched Mom take care of you in those years after the accident. I know someone is here in a spiritual body, but I'm not sure who you are—Jesus, angel, Dad, or Grandma.*

I'm trying everything to stop the ulcers. Numb, I felt I didn't know what to do anymore. I took Mom's supplies off the dresser and turned back to care for her feet. I wrapped each toe, but discovered purple quarter-sized spots beginning to form on the tops of her knees.

As I worked on Mom, I considered how heavenly beings gave me strength to go on. Without speaking a word, they assured me: *We're here for you, Diane.*

Sometimes my only relief came from thinking about childhood memories. After lunch that same day, I stood by the kitchen sink rinsing the dishes and stemware for the dishwasher. While I reminisced about growing up, I gazed through the window at a sparrow drinking from a water puddle.

Going through puberty hadn't been easy. I felt heavy and ugly, but I loved to act, sing, and dance. I was in love with James Dean, the actor. His pictures covered the walls of my room, and I joined his fan club. At the time, the girls wore skirts and sweaters with colorful little neck scarves and penny loafers with bobby socks. I remembered a particular evening when Mom and Dad prepared to go out dancing with their friends.

Dad came into the living room where I listened to music. "Diane, your mother's still dressing. Can you button my shirt and make sure my bow tie is straight?"

"Sure, Dad."

The stereo was playing Wayne King's music, and Dad began singing. When he was in the band, Dad and Mom never had a chance to dance because he performed, singing or playing the drums.

After I straightened then reattached the metal clasp on his collar, Dad took my arm and we started dancing. His steps were easy to follow. How I'd loved dancing with him!

Just then, Mom walked into the living room. We stopped dancing and turned to look at her. She wore an elegant navy off-the-shoulder taffeta dress. Her glowing hair crowned her head in soft curls and waves. She turned slowly, stopping with her back to us; layers of soft white eyelet cascaded in ruffles from waist to hem. She smiled and looked at us sideways as if posing for a picture. My father whistled the entire time she pirouetted. She was stunning.

When she faced us Dad said, "You look beautiful, Donna."

"You look so beautiful," I repeated. "Mom, that's a beautiful dress." I hesitated. "You look like someone; I can't place it, but you look like . . ."

"Lucille Ball?" Dad asked.

"Yes, you look like Lucy!"

I wanted so badly to be slender, small enough to wear that dress. By the time I could slip into it, styles had changed, of course, and the navy taffeta had turned purple in spots.

Later that afternoon, I stood at the doorway of Mom's room; she was sleeping soundly. Yes, the navy taffeta was her dress forever.

Through visits from Heaven and signs from God during my mother's long illness, I was given the strength to understand God's intention. Soon I'd receive more signs from Him through my spiritual mentor, Barbara Allen.

CHAPTER EIGHT:
THE VISIT

Look for signs from God

I opened the screen door and stuck my head out. It was sprinkling earlier, but the day had brightened, leaving only a few clouds dotting the light blue sky. When I stepped onto the sidewalk leading to the backyard, a small white butterfly fluttering among the foliage caught my eye. It danced before me and I held my hand out.

"Hi, you delicate little thing." Immediately, I thought of my friend and mentor, Barbara Allen. Her spiritual symbol was the butterfly.

After backing my two-tone brown Pontiac out of the garage to drive uptown that day in 1987, I noticed each manicured lawn I passed was bright green. And the flowers were perky and brilliant since the rain shower. When I turned onto Maple Street, a white butterfly flew up and hovered over the hood of the car. It paused in mid-air for a moment, fluttering its tiny wings as if trying to get my attention. Then it skittered away, zigzagging on air currents and over invisible obstacles.

Once I'd asked Barbara Allen why she chose the butterfly as her symbol. She explained the meaning. "It's a sign of immortality. The caterpillar appears to die, but . . ." Her eyes sparkled and her words about the caterpillar-to-butterfly metamorphosis seemed all the more intriguing.

Years earlier, Barbara Allen mentioned her five near-death experiences at the first self-awareness class I took with her. She told us that the vibratory frequency of her near-death situations increased with each experience and her personality seemed to alter as she grew emotionally, mentally, and spiritually through each event.

It seemed appropriate that the butterfly was Barbara Allen's symbol because she always referred to herself as a gypsy, moving from place to place within a six to twelve month period following each near-death episode. Like a traveling performer, she reinvented herself by moving, delving into new occupations, and forming new friendships. Simultaneously, she experienced greater dedication to the universe in her renewed life.

It was three years since Barbara Allen left the Chicago area to live with her family in South Carolina. For Valentine's Day she sent me a small box dotted with little butterfly stickers. She had drawn a chrysanthemum on the box in red ink with the word PAX beneath it, meaning peace. The box held a book called *Jonathan Livingston Seagull* and an audiocassette tape.

When I received Barbara Allen's package, I slipped the tape into a cassette player. When Neil Diamond's music filled the room, I opened the book to the first page. Out flew a colored photograph of a large white seagull in flight. The inscription read, "For my sister of the spirit. Our souls are aware of each other. Like Jonathan, we are One in a Million."

By the time I finished the little book, I knew why Barbara Allen had sent it. All these years, she'd cultivated and nurtured me with one thing in mind. She wanted to prepare me to teach what I'd learned at her side. I no longer needed her as my mentor, for now I knew all she had to teach. She prepared me for the day when she would take flight, as Jonathan had done when he'd left Fletcher Seagull. Her job as my teacher was completed, for I'd become my own teacher.

Years later, after I wrote about my own near-death experience, Barbara Allen said,

"It was no accident that I came into your life. You've always known our relationship was different, that we were different. Now we know why. We have more in common than you thought. When I first met you, I knew that I was supposed to nurture, teach, love, and care for you. I told you, Diane, you can write. You are a writer!

A good teacher lets the student come into the knowledge on her own.

In the fall, I learned that my friend had been hospitalized in South Carolina. Barbara Allen had been persistently ill for several years, but this time her illness lasted longer than expected. Fragile, she had difficulty breathing and was so ill she couldn't speak. I sent her an angel pin to wear on her shoulder.

Two weeks before Christmas, I went to a card shop to look for a special card for her. I found a most unusual card with a Christmas tree in a desert scene. The branches of the tree were made of multicolored butterfly wings. Later that evening, as I studied the picture, I composed a little story and penned it onto the blank page inside:

> *There are so many wondrous things on God's earth—trees, flowers, birds, and so much more. In the winter, if you live in the northern hemisphere, the land is covered with a blanket of snow. Our flowers die, most of our birds fly south, and our trees are bare except for the snow that blankets their branches.*
>
> *There is a legend of a beautiful tree in a faraway land that only blooms at Christmas time. It reminds us of all God has created during the year. It is said that long ago during the flight of Mary, Joseph, and the Babe to Egypt, they rested near a tree one evening. Mary washed Jesus' clothing and hung it on the branches to dry. Since that time, each tree branch blooms with flowers of different colors shaped like giant butterfly wings.*
>
> *And so this Christmas, my dear friend, I greet you, not quite as other people greet one another, but with a story that came to mind as I held this lovely card.*

One day, some time after Barbara Allen recovered from her illness, Mom slept while I watched television in our living room with my feet up. I heard a flapping noise. I looked around the room to see where the sound came from. The Sunday papers lay near the heating vent, the pages flapping and flying above it. It sounded like large wings, large enough to support angels as they flew through the air. For me, signs from God were reflected in everyday symbols, thoughts, or flashes of intuition.

The next day I received an audiocassette tape from Barbara Allen. She said, "I just got airline tickets to come to Chicago next month."

Now I understood the meaning of those flapping wing sounds the newspapers had made.

It was the third week in April 1988 when Barbara Allen arrived at our home. We greeted each other as old friends do, but this time I cried when I saw her.

"Oh, I'm so glad you came." I put my arms around her. "It's so good to see you again." I rested my head on her shoulder. "It's been . . . it's been . . ." I was crying so much I couldn't finish my sentence.

"I know, Diane, I know. I'm here now." She gently patted my back.

She'd nursed her own mother through an illness. After a few moments, I asked her if she'd like to see my mom. When Mom came to live with us we converted our television room into a temporary bedroom. As we entered the room, Mom turned her head toward us from her hospital bed.

"Hi, Donna," Barbara Allen said softly. "I have something for you. I hope you like it."

She gave Mom one of her beautiful crocheted bed jackets and wished Mom well, holding her hand for a few moments. Mom nodded her thanks with a glowing smile.

That evening we had dinner out. I parked the car in the restaurant lot, turned to Barbara Allen and asked, "What do you think about my mom?"

She looked slightly apprehensive and gave me a soft, but direct answer. "There seems to be very little life force in her. I felt that when I touched her hand."

Barbara Allen's empathy touched me deeply. I loved my friend so much because she was part of me: my earth angel, my teacher and my sister of the spirit.

Later that evening, she took pictures of Valerie, Lloyd and me as we opened the gifts she'd brought. Valerie got her camera out too, and while Barbara Allen posed, I admired the white jumpsuit she wore.

Barbara Allen picked up two little boxes. "These are for you, Diane."

The first gift I opened was a lovely crystal pendant on a gold chain. When I opened the second box, I was speechless. There amidst the colorful tissue paper lay a handmade, white butterfly pin. Its meaning, I knew, was immortality.

Signs from God heightened my sense of touch, sight, and hearing. Soon I'd learn to use my spiritual love unconditionally.

CHAPTER NINE: IN THE PALM OF HIS HAND

Take comfort in knowing there is life beyond death

One morning I walked through the hallway and turned to look into Mom's bedroom. She was sleeping, and the framed wedding photograph on her nightstand reflected a warm glow from the lamplight. I entered the room and gazed down at her. Her red hair had started to reveal the gray she'd once tried so feverishly to hide. I leaned over her to see if she breathed freely, then my eyes returned to the photograph.

I spoke to Dad silently. *Remember when you and I watched "The Ghost and Mrs. Muir" before you died? I know you're waiting for Mom. When you come for her, will it be like the movie? Will you look as young as you were in the picture? Will your spirit brush past me, as you and Mom walk hand-in-hand out the door? Will I be alone to discover her body?*

For the past three days, whenever I went into Mom's room, I found her looking up at the ceiling.

"Mom, what are you looking at?" I stood at the end of the bed and followed her line of sight. When I gazed back at her, her face glowed softly. I looked up, too, and sensed a presence.

An apparition stood at the foot of her bed, a man five feet ten inches or taller, about the height of my father. I sensed his form, but I couldn't quite make out the details. Mom seemed to be in a trance, so I walked to the side of the bed and shook her gently.

"Mom, Mom," I called softly. Finally, she turned her head and looked at me. "It's time for your pills, Mom." I turned toward the doorway and wondered if I was really seeing Dad, and looked back at her. "I'll just be a few minutes." I headed for the kitchen to prepare our breakfast, wondering if heavenly beings would walk right through me when they came for her.

Valerie came home for lunch at noon. She told me about an unusual dream she had the night before. "I stood in Grandma's bedroom. There wasn't any furniture in the room except an ironing board. Outside Grandma's bedroom door, there was a line of people. They all handed me greeting cards, but I couldn't figure out why. Even the guys I sing with in the band were handing me cards. I looked at one of them. There on gold foil it said, "Dear Grandmother."

By now, Valerie had my full attention.

"Then the dream switched to you, Daddy, and me getting into a limousine. Rita was with us, but I couldn't figure out why she should be going somewhere with us. The limo had three doors. What do you think, Mom?"

When I heard the dream, I knew my mother's time was near but I didn't tell Valerie. "Oh, I don't know . . . what I *do* know is that if anything happens to Grandma, I want Rita in the family car. She's Grandma's niece and godchild."

That night I had an interesting dream myself. My father's friend, Joe, who died the previous year, looked at me so seriously that I woke up at 3:00 in the morning. I wandered into the kitchen for a glass of milk and sat down to think. Why would Joe appear in my dream? Then I remembered his birthday, April 30. Today was April 28. But surely, I thought, if anything was going to happen to Mom, the signs would be stronger. Even Valerie's dream wasn't the elaborate type she usually had.

The next morning I got up late. I had slept so soundly I hadn't heard the alarm go off. I peeked into Mom's room. She heard me and turned her head toward the doorway.

"Good morning, Mom." She smiled when I walked into the room. I began washing her face, but she pushed me away with her good hand. Her expression made it clear she didn't want me to fuss with her today. Her breathing was different, more labored than usual. When preparing her breakfast, I cut her food in small pieces. Easier for her to swallow, I thought.

After Mom finished breakfast, I found Lloyd sitting at the kitchen table. I sat near him. "Good morning, Hon."

"Good morning?" he asked with surprise. "It's almost afternoon! I'll be in the garage if you want me, Diane. It's time to rotate the car's tires."

"Mom doesn't look good," I told him. "Her breathing seems more labored."

Lloyd headed for the back door, then turned and looked at me. "Call me if you need me."

I went into the bathroom to finish dressing and heard my father singing *Diane*, one of three songs he performed at my wedding reception. I didn't realize then that he was coming back for my mother. I stood in front of the mirror a long time, remembering Dad's powerful rendition of *Diane*. The song had emotionally affected family and friends. My friend Jane briefly recounted her reaction many times when we spoke about my father. "Your father sang the song like he had written it for you. He even introduced the song as *My Diane*. When I glanced around the room, everyone was teary-eyed. All your friends at our table were crying. Each of us knew we'd never have our father display his love for us on our wedding day like your father did for you."

I was eighteen when Lloyd and I married. Lloyd was so handsome with his dark, wavy hair, deep blue eyes, and gentle nature that I couldn't help but love him. On our wedding day, I finally became the beauty I'd always dreamed about. The v-neckline and fitted waist of my white peau de soie gown revealed my hourglass figure. A large crown of borealis crystals to grace my head completed the princess attire. As I stood in the church's foyer, waiting to walk down the aisle, my great-aunt Dot admired me.

"I've seen many brides, Diane, but none radiated the loving glow you have on your face today. You're just beautiful." She moved into the sanctuary as my father came toward me.

"Ready?" he asked.

"Yes, Dad," I murmured, looking up into his proud but teary eyes.

As the organ rumbled into the stirring strains of the wedding march, we walked down the aisle on the white runner. Some of my relatives turned in their pews to look at me. They smiled, and I smiled back at them. When I looked toward the altar, the vague outline of the head of Christ appeared on the wall above and behind it. Apparently no one else saw this apparition. I was so taken by the image, I almost forgot to kiss Dad when we arrived at the front of the sanctuary.

When I looked back into the mirror, there were tears in my eyes. I finished applying my lipstick and headed for the kitchen, remembering Lloyd would leave for work at 3:30 that afternoon. I decided to call Mom's girlfriend, Sandy. I told her Mom's condition worsened overnight and asked her to come over. But she was ill too, and couldn't stay with me.

The night before, when I'd finally dropped off to sleep, I asked God to hold her in the palm of His hand. I lit the candle on the kitchen stovetop and prayed to God again. I asked Him to take my mom and tell her that I loved her. I couldn't watch her suffer any more.

I tiptoed into the hallway and looked into Mom's bedroom as I'd done so many times before. She was looking up at the wall again, her mouth open and her light skin almost transparent.

I hurried into the room. "Mom. Mom. Oh, my God!"

The oxygen tank sat near the bed. I grabbed for it but fumbled and couldn't turn it on. I opened the window and yelled to Lloyd, still out in the garage. "Lloyd, get in here fast!"

Within seconds, he sprinted up the stairs and turned the valve of the oxygen tank. Mom wasn't breathing. I picked her hand up and patted it. She was gone. God had heard my cries. He'd waited for me to let go.

We held Mom's wake the next day, April 29, and we buried her on April 30—Joe's birthday. As we prepared for the funeral, Valerie went with us to order floral arrangements. She wanted the florist to spell out Granny, her special name for her grandmother, on white ribbon decorating the flowers. The florist could only hand print the name on the ribbon, and tried convincing Valerie that it looked more professional if she'd choose a ribbon that said "Dear Grandmother" in gold-foil lettering.

When we walked out of the funeral home the next day, another piece of Valerie's dream materialized. A limousine waited to take us to the cemetery. Valerie nudged me. "Look at the limo, Mom. It has three doors."

I shot a look at Valerie, realizing all the parts of her dream had occurred. Her cinnamon-colored hair gleamed into a flaming auburn in the sunlight. She had lost weight during these difficult months, becoming more beautiful as she grew older. She looks so much like my mother, I thought.

Rita, Valerie, Lloyd and I entered the limousine. "Everyone is saying what a saint you are, Di," Rita said. "Is there a Saint Diane?" She paused. "There will be," she added sincerely.

"Rita, I'm not even Catholic."

Lloyd touched my hand. "You have nothing to be ashamed of, Diane. No regrets," he said with emotion.

Lloyd, so quietly handsome. I looked out of the limousine window as we pulled up to the gravesite and I remembered my father's words. Years ago, Dad described Lloyd as "a prince of a man."

After Lloyd and I went to bed that night, I had a vision. I saw my parents standing on a puffy blue and white cloud. The head of Christ at their side was covered in a white mist, radiating a brilliant light over them. My father was dressed in the navy-blue suit with the fine white stripe in which he was buried, and my mother wore her mauve dress with the pleated skirt and long, chiffon sleeves fashioned with little pink pearl buttons. Dad had an arm around her waist, and she had her arm around his. Both of them waved at me. Their beauty cannot be described. I was careful not to speak, remembering how my father had so quickly disappeared the first time he'd visited me. The scene filled me with the glow of love. I smiled. They were with God, in Heaven together. One tear rolled from the corner of my eye and across the bridge of my nose. I lay at peace, drinking in this beautiful vision, knowing I was seeing the face of Christ as I had on my wedding day twenty-six years earlier.

I received Heaven's unconditional help to accept my mother's death. Now, through gifts of remembrance, the circle of life continued.

Chapter Ten :
The Christmas Angel

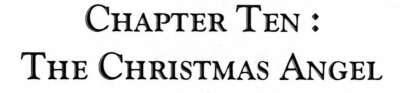

Life is a circle

A few days after my mother's death, I received a package from Barbara Allen. She hadn't sent flowers, she wrote, because they die so quickly. Instead, she sent a music box displaying a small angel doll dressed in white and trimmed in gold. Her metallic cloth wings wrapped loosely around her body in a cocoon of gold. In her hands she cradled a white butterfly nestled on a golden rose. Barbara mentioned in her sympathy card that she wanted to send that particular angel not as a remembrance of death but of life, eternal life, and hoped I didn't mind that the music box played a holiday song. I stood in our living room holding the angel and turned the wheel at the base of its stand. Then I set it down on the piano and watched her pirouette slowly to the strains of *Hark the Herald Angels Sing*. Barbara Allen had sent a Christmas angel.

Every year at Christmas I unwrapped Barbara Allen's music box angel, held her in my hands and turned the wheel at its base. Then I'd set her down and watch her pirouette to the music as I had the first time, savoring old memories.

The Christmas angel reminded me of a surprising intervention from Heaven. In 1979, I would produce, direct, and act in *The Christmas Angel,* the first play ever performed in Little City.

Late in the summer, my neighborhood girlfriend and schoolmate, Ellen, and her ten-year-old daughter Ruthie were due to arrive at our house from their home in Chicago. We had planned to perform a Christmas musical for a group we felt would enjoy watching a live production. Valerie, by then an energetic teenager who enjoyed acting in high school musicals, was interested in performing with us. Her voice and its smooth alto range would be an asset to our little group.

I made an appointment for December 16 at a school for mentally and emotionally challenged children in the town of Palatine for the "Tillman and Company Players." Ellen, Ruthie, Valerie, and I worked on music, props, and costumes every week through the fall. While I prepared the costumes and decorated them, Valerie gathered props and painted them. By the last week of rehearsal, everything was finished except the angel wings. Sitting on the floor of the living room next to the piano, I made wings from gold-foil wrapping paper and trimmed them with golden garland.

At last, a cold and snowy December 16 arrived. Ellen and Ruth would come from the city and meet us in Palatine. I loaded the trunk and back seat of our '71 Oldsmobile, packing them full of stage equipment and costumes. Valerie and I both climbed into the car, and we backed out of the garage onto streets covered with ice. Happily, the props weighed the car down.

I drove about twenty miles to the expressway, hoping the pavement wasn't slick like the surface roads. But it proved to be slippery. When we approached an incline in the road, I looked at the speedometer; we traveled a conservative fifteen miles an hour. As we started up the incline, the car spun around without warning and kept on turning.

Valerie's voice was taut with fear. "We're going to die!"

"Oh, no, we're not!" I tried to remember how to straighten a spinning car. I looked over my left shoulder and saw a fifteen-foot drop.

Oh, God, I silently prayed.

My hands gripped the steering wheel, but I had an uncanny feeling that some power other than mine rotated it. The car stopped turning as suddenly as it had started, and we faced the direction from

70

which we had come. Cars in both directions on the highway stopped and waited about two hundred yards in front and behind us.

I sat still for a moment, shaken, then slowly turned the car around. "Boy, for a minute there, I thought we'd die."

"But you said we wouldn't die," Valerie protested.

I almost laughed. She'd caught me. "Yes, God knows we're on our way with something special for the children. He wants us to do *The Christmas Angel.*"

Barbara Allen's Christmas angel brought back memories of my mother and the Christmas angel she gave me for my fourteenth birthday.

One snowy afternoon in the winter of 1956, Mom called me from the kitchen. "Diane, they're selling Christmas trees at a lot near Harlem and Belmont Avenues. How would you like to help me pick out our tree this year?"

I knew she couldn't manage alone. Dad used the car on Saturdays for transportation to the restaurant and back. Mom never drove a car.

"Sure, but how do we get it home?" I asked, walking into the kitchen.

"Well, I thought you'd go out to the chicken coop." She referred to the miniature storage shed Grandma Verda kept her rabbits and chickens in during World War II. "We could use your sled to carry the tree. Later, we'll decorate it with old ornaments. Remember the tinsel I made you save last year? We can use it again."

"Oh, no," I said loudly.

"We saved tinsel during the depression and we saved it during the war."

"But, Mom, it's only ten cents!"

"A penny saved is a dollar earned."

"But, Mom."

"You'll see. We'll have a real old-fashioned Christmas."

We took turns pulling the empty sled on the snow-covered streets, walking in tire tracks made by cars and trucks. Wherever possible, Mom and I used the sidewalk, packed down with layers of snow from previous storms, to make the sled glide easier.

"Diane, breathe into your muffler. It'll keep your chest warm. You have to take care of that cough."

I wrapped the long scarf around my nose and mouth and groaned. "Yes, Mother."Lagging behind the sled, I watched her determination to have an old-fashioned Christmas. When she turned around, swirling snowflakes dotted her red hair and she glistened.

"Come on, Diane. We're almost there."

At the lot, the salesman tied the tree to the sled. We chose a five-foot Douglas pine. At home, we carried the tree up the enclosed back staircase to the second floor.

I went into the kitchen to make a cup of hot chocolate. A few minutes later, Mom came into the room and handed me a small wrapped gift.

"This is yours, Diane." Mom turned toward the liquor cabinet to make herself a Manhattan.

I unwrapped the box carefully, exposing a lovely Christmas figurine.

Mom returned with the drink in her hand. "Happy fourteenth birthday!" She held her glass up to toast me.

"It's an angel!"

The figurine, dressed in a winter costume from the eighteenth century, wore light green and carried homemade gifts in her arms. Highly polished gold angel wings shaped like hearts jutted out from each side of her back. A half-halo the color of her wings hovered at the back of her head.

"You're my Christmas angel." Mom gave me a hug and thanked me for taking two weeks off from school to help at the restaurant. During Thanksgiving she'd suffered from a bout of double pneumonia, and Dad had an attack of spinal rheumatoid arthritis. Neither one of my parents could get out of bed. The emergency left me helping their employees while Dad's aged mother became hostess and supervised the entire restaurant operation.

After my father's death during the winter of 1976, Mom closed the restaurant every night. She checked the daily receipts, waited for the employees to finish their jobs, and gave the stainless steel equipment an extra polishing. When all was secure, she called a taxi company and sat in a booth near the front picture window to wait.

It was almost 10:30 one snowy December night when I finished making a couple of pumpkin pies. I'd used the extra pastry to top each pie with a small cookie in the shape of a Christmas tree.

I lifted the pies out of the oven and placed them on the stovetop. The telephone rang.

"Diane, my cab hasn't picked me up. Do you think you could come get me?"

"You're still at the restaurant and you didn't call me?"

"I didn't think the storm would be this bad, but with the thirteen inches from yesterday and snow tonight, I guess they just couldn't come for me."

"Mom, cancel your cab. I'll be right there." I hung the telephone back on the kitchen wall and strode down the hall to the television room.

"Val, I'm going to pick Grandma up at the restaurant. She can't get a cab to take her home."

"Mom, you're not going to drive, are you? The weatherman just told everyone to stay inside. It's bad out there."

"No, I'm not going to drive. Your dad took the car to work, in case they asked him to stay over and plow the parking lot. You and I are going to walk to the restaurant and bring Grandma back to our house. Do you still have your saucer sled?"

"It's in the garage. Mom, if you're thinking what I'm thinking, Grandma's not going to use a sled."

"No, she probably won't but we better take it along. She might change her mind. You never know."

We got the red saucer sled from the garage and walked out the gate onto snow-covered sidewalks and streets. The north wind, coupled with the blowing snow, swirled into high drifts on one side of the sidewalk. On Grand Avenue, cars sat motionless. Two snowmobiles weaved in and out of stalled traffic.

When we arrived at the restaurant, Mom was sitting in a booth near the front window. She rose when she heard the tapping of my keys against the thick glass door.

"I wondered what happened to you," she said, smiling.

"It took longer than the usual twenty minutes to get here."

"Where's the car?" Mom peered out the window.

"Lloyd has it."

"You're kidding. No, really. Where's the car?"

"We walked here, Mom."

Valerie held up her red plastic saucer sled. "Here, Granny, we brought this along for you. We're going to pull you down Grand Avenue on my sled." Val laughed.

"Valerie, stop laughing like that, it sounds forced. You'll never get a man to marry you with a crazy laugh like that."

I turned back to my mother. "I'm sorry Mom, this is the best we could do."

"I'll stay here tonight."

"Don't be silly! You're coming to our house. Besides, you'll scare your morning crew half to death if they see you sleeping in a booth."

Mom fell silent.

"Come on, Granny Goose. Don't be silly," Valerie chuckled.

"Okay, but I'm not going to sit in that sled."

I glanced at Valerie, who smiled with an "I told you so" look.

"I've made some homemade pumpkin pies. They should've cooled off by now. You can sleep on the sofa. In the morning, I'll take you home."

The three of us trudged along snow-covered sidewalks, crossing side streets until we reached the intersection at Grand Avenue.

"How are you doing, Mom?" I shouted against the wind.

"Okay."

"How are your feet holding up? You've been on them all day."

"They feel like two stumps."

I watched her walking next to me. Mom's scarf was wrapped loosely around her nose and mouth. A tear rolled down her cheek. I leaned over and felt the weight of her purse.

"Mom, what's in your purse? It must weigh a ton."

"Daily receipts and some extra rolls of quarters, dimes and pennies."

"Let me carry it for awhile." I worried about the extra strain on her heart. "If you won't let me carry your purse, how about making my life easier by sitting in the sled and holding both our purses? Come on, you can do it."

Valerie pulled the empty sled ahead of us. She turned near the railroad tracks and yelled. "Come on, you two, we're almost there."

"Val," I yelled, "bring your sled back here. Grandma's going to sit in it while I pull her home."

Val trudged back to us and set her sled down on the snowy sidewalk. "I gotta see this," she mumbled.

Mom sat her purse in the snow while I helped her into the saucer sled. She held both purses on her lap, her legs jutting out in front of her as she gripped the side of the sled for balance.

When we reached the house, it was 11:30. The light from the kitchen fell against the snowdrifts in the front yard and it sparkled.

"Welcome to our small abode, Mother." I bowed and held the front door open for her. The smell of the freshly baked pumpkin pies lingered in the air, adding spice to our yuletide spirit. Valerie rushed ahead of us to her bedroom.

"You have your tree decorated in old-fashioned ornaments this year."

"Valerie's idea; she wanted an old-fashioned Christmas."

I eased Mom's coat from her shoulders and hung it in the hall closet.

"You still have the angel?" She noticed the Christmas angel she had given me on the coffee table.

"Yes, I put her out every year. She always reminds me of the time we trudged through the snow for a Christmas tree on my birthday. Remember when we started decorating it and found a nest hidden in the branches?"

"Yes, I remember. There were four white eggs with little blue speckles, close to hatching. Something must have happened to the mother bird earlier that year. You took the eggs from the nest and replaced them with Easter candy eggs."

"Do you remember what you told me, Mom? You said, 'It's a gift from God. A reminder that all things, great and small, renew themselves. Life goes on, because nothing ever really dies'."

The next morning when I turned on the car radio on the way to Mom's house, the weatherman gave his morning report. He mentioned an accident involving several cars and a taxicab at 11:00 p.m. the night before in Franklin Park, a few blocks from Mom's house.

"Mom, did you hear that?"

"Listen," she whispered.

The weatherman continued his story. ". . . The taxicab from O'Hare Airport was traveling southbound near the intersection of Mannheim Road and Grand Avenue when the driver, whose name is being withheld until further investigation, lost control of his vehicle. The taxicab jumped the median and skidded into several cars in the northbound lane of traffic."

Mom looked at me. "What time was it when you came to the restaurant to pick me up?

"I don't know. You called me at 10:30 and it takes twenty minutes to walk to the restaurant. Give or take five to ten minutes because of the storm. Why?"

"Nothing, it's probably a coincidence, but I'll always wonder if it's the same taxicab I canceled before you and Valerie got to the restaurant."

"Well, coincidence or not . . ." I paused a moment. "A higher power seems to be involved, because you weren't riding in a taxicab or our car. It's obvious someone went to great lengths to get Valerie and me safely to the restaurant and back to our house with you in tow."

I glanced at Mom, sitting next to me in the front seat. She didn't reply and appeared to be deep in thought. We passed a manger scene sitting on the roof of a church. Last night's storm had blown most of the figures down.

As we came closer to the scene, Mom thrust her hand up and pointed out the front windshield. "Diane, look at the Christmas angel!"

I looked where she pointed. "That's strange. With His arms raised up and out of the manger, doesn't it look like Baby Jesus is ordering His angel to protect us as we drive down the street?" [3]

"Maybe so, Diane, but you better drive a little faster before that angel falls down and hits the car."

"Do you want me to floor it?" I imitated my father, glancing at her with eye-popping glee.

---

[3] Refers to Psalms 91: 11-12. "For He shall give his angels charge over thee to keep thee in all thy ways. They shall bear thee up in their hands lest thou dash thy foot against a stone."

The following Monday at the restaurant, after the lunch hour had ended, I went back through the kitchen and into the storage room. Mom was sitting behind the desk, talking on the telephone to one of the suppliers. When I walked around the desk, I noticed a large package sitting on the floor next to her. After a few moments she hung up the telephone.

"What's in the package?" I asked.

"Oh. Uh," she stammered, "A sleeping bag."

"Oh, no . . ."

The fading music box rendition of Hark the Herald Angels Sing brought me back to the present. I looked again at Barbara Allen's Christmas angel pirouetting on the piano. She stopped rotating and faced the Christmas tree. The lights caught the gold trim on her gown and she twinkled in the silence of the night.

The circle of life turned once again through my memories of past Christmases. Now the incredible presence of the One who helped me would manifest through a Thanksgiving memory.

CHAPTER ELEVEN: A JOB WELL DONE

Give without expectations

I was preparing dinner a week after Mom's death when I suddenly had the irrepressible urge to hum one of my father's songs. I closed my eyes, greeting him in my mind. He stood before me on the stairway leading into the kitchen.

Dad, I didn't think you'd come back.

I wanted to tell you how much I care, Dad replied. *I'm happy that the long siege with Mom's illness is over.*

For seventeen years he'd helped by giving me the support of his music and lyrics, and by waiting faithfully for Mom.

Oh, Dad, I love you. Please stay here with us, I begged. *Are you coming back some time?*

He patted me on the shoulder and seemed to float down the stairs and out the doorway. *I'm not sure, Diane. Be happy. You have a special gift with the spiritual world. You've used it wisely. I love you and I'm proud of you. A job well done.*

Dad always spoke those familiar words when I'd done something he liked: *A job well done.*

In the fall of 1957, a few weeks before Thanksgiving, Dad brought a small paper bag home to Grandma Verda's two-story house on Octavia Street. A customer at the restaurant had given it to him, and now he handed the paper bag to me.

"This is for you, Diane. Let's see what kind of a job you can do with him."

I opened the bag and peered into it. "It's a bird!"

Dad warned me to be careful, that the little bird might be frightened from being in the paper bag and try to bite me. He added that he wasn't sure, but it was possible that the bird may have been damaged to begin with. He explained that one of the customers raised parakeets and had so many that he started to give them away. The customer had asked if he knew of anyone who could take care of one of his birds.

I retrieved Grandma Verda's canary cage from the basement storage room, carried it upstairs and placed it on the kitchen counter next to the paper bag. Every time I put my hand in the bag the blue and white bird tried to bite me. I grabbed one of Dad's leather gloves from the counter and tried transferring the little parakeet to the cage again. He bit down hard on the leather glove, his beak clinging to the young girl attempting to change his life.

I peered into his cage, watching him constantly. I placed an extra perch under his breast. He resisted, flying wildly from perch to perch and to the sidebars of his cage. A few hours passed, and finally the bird sat silently on his perch. I tried to get him to trust me again. This time, I put a silver nickel up to his beak. He grabbed it and held on.

"Dad, look at the parakeet holding a nickel in his beak!"

Dad leaned down and peered into the cage. "Looks like you have a job ahead of you, training this bird."

Early on Thanksgiving afternoon, I went downstairs into the dining room that had been converted into a small, open television room for Grams after the accident. She sat on the sofa, her legs jutting out in front of her, crossed at the ankle. I couldn't help but notice how her homemade dress of fall colors blended into the orange vinyl sofa.

"Dawling, don't we look fallish today," I quipped in a Bette Davis drawl as I sat down beside her.

Just then, my step-grandfather Harry entered the kitchen from the back door and walked into the television room.

"Hi, Picklepuss," he greeted me, and I smiled as he leaned over Grams and gave her a kiss on the cheek.

Almost as if on cue, Dad entered the room from the front hall entrance. "Happy Thanksgiving!" he crowed. He carried pumpkin pies atop a large cardboard box of bottled alcohol and soda mixes for the party.

"Happy Thanksgiving!" we replied as he walked past us into the kitchen and placed the boxes on the table.

"Ed, would you like a drink?" Harry asked. "I was just about to make one for myself."

"Don't mind if I do."

While Grandpa and Dad were in the kitchen, Grams turned to me. "Your Aunt Dot's friend Trudy telephoned me this morning. Trudy said she and Mike couldn't get over you visiting with Mike's mother last week. Especially since his mother doesn't understand English, and you don't understand Polish. They're elated that you gave her all your attention. She's a very lonely old woman with no one to talk with. Trudy says she's overlooked by their friends much of the time. How in the world did you do that?" Grandma smiled, her eyebrows raised in surprise.

"I didn't have any trouble, Grams, we understood each other. I enjoyed being with Mike's mother, really I did. We played cards, smiled a lot, and she showed me the little things in her room that she'd collected."

"Trudy says Mike's mother keeps asking, 'Where's that girl? Where's that girl'?"

Filled with a sense of pride that the little Polish lady had asked for me, I smiled with contentment.

Grams placed her hand on my arm and patted it. "Well, that was a very kind thing you did for his mother, sweetheart. I told Trudy how you helped all of us after the accident. You were such a little girl then. You'd collect all the bedpans and urinals, empty them and rinse them out, and lay them near us for the next time we needed them."

"Grams, you didn't tell Trudy that?" I asked, embarrassed. I looked up as Harry walked into the television room and sat down across from us. Dad stood at the doorway with his jacket folded over one arm, holding the drink that Grandpa Harry had made for him. I didn't know how long they'd been listening to us from the kitchen.

"I didn't mean to embarrass you by telling you this," Grams continued. "I told Trudy about the hardships I put you through after the accident, and how you rode your bicycle to the corner grocer for the little things I needed."

"Grams, the whole family helped you. I didn't do it alone. When Rita was better, she helped you, too," I reminded her.

"Yes, my entire family helped. They'd do anything for us, and I'd do anything for them. We're a very loving family. But they're adults; you were a child. After Rita moved away, you were a comfort to me, staying with me, doing those small things I couldn't do. I depended a lot on you. You never complained or begrudged me anything. I was harder on you than you could ever be on me."

Everyone was speechless as we listened to Grandma Verda.

"Remember when Harry drove you and me to the department store when I wanted to buy a winter coat?"

I nodded.

"I felt ashamed and uncomfortable with my crutch under my arm, but you put it on the floor in the back seat of the car and extended your arm for me to hold. Harry and others had helped me many times before; it wasn't just that kindly gesture. In the store I hobbled next to you, holding your arm. We made it to the coat rack and you said loudly, imitating a movie star, 'I think you should really buy a pair of shoes, Dawling! Ever since you bought those little black pumps, you limp something awful'."

"I knew what you were doing. You drew everyone's attention to me and turned my disability into nothing more than a pinched foot." She paused. "You were never ashamed of me. Instead, you walked proudly beside me. I never saw anything like it."

Harry, sitting directly across from me, noticed my eyes misting and interrupted her. "Say, Picklepuss, are you still using a leather glove on the bird your father gave you?"

"No, I took the glove off last week. He flies all over the house now, sits on my finger. When the cage door is open, he flies to the hall, landing to greet Dad and me. He sits on our shoulders, gives us a kiss and nibbles on our ears. He tickles me! He's not frightened any more and he loves me," I told him.

"That's amazing how you turned the bird around like that. We all thought he was damaged," Harry said.

"See, that's what I mean," Grams added. "You took that helpless bird, cared for him, did everything for him, and he became a sweet, loving bird. Something is different about you. Taking care of others comes natural to you. You accept and give refuge to the tragedies, sufferings, and problems of others. You do it without any thought of yourself."

"Grams, I don't do anything different than anyone else."

"Oh, but you *do* do something different," she sternly said. "You're so pure in heart you can't see it." [4]

Pure in heart. Grams had never said that about me before. I was surprised and had to think about what she was saying.

"I've seen you do this for everyone, and you never ask for anything in return. You know, people like to receive a gift for their services, but you never seem to feel that way. You're the most unselfish child I've ever known."

My father peered at me from the doorway. "I think what your grandmother is saying is that all the things you've done without any thought of yourself have had a greater effect on you than you've realized."

"She's a humanitarian?" Harry blurted out.

"No, she's more than a humanitarian," Dad replied.

"Well, Picklepuss, I don't care what you are or what you'll become, but I'd like to have a patent on it," Harry said. "Then I'd like to pickle it and bottle it for all time."

"Harry, I think someone else has the patent on this one," Dad said. "You know, Donna and I saw a movie a few years ago at the Montclair Theater about a doctor motivated by love. He performed surgeries no one else could perform. When the patient was ready to pay the bill, he wouldn't charge them for his services. The only thing he asked of them was they not tell anyone he didn't charge them for the operation. In this way, he continued performing operations no one else could do. He found the charity of his giving enabled him to tap into a higher power."

Just then my mom called from the upstairs hallway. "Well, I'd better see what Donna wants," Dad said, walking past us. "Diane has similar qualities, don't you think? Her strength will be found in her

---

[4] Refers to Matthew 5:8, King James version. "Blessed are the pure in heart, for they shall see God."

kindness toward others." He smiled and nodded comically with a lifted brow, one eye shut in a long wink.

A few minutes later, still smiling, Dad peeked around the hall entrance into Grandma's apartment. With a look of pride on his face he said, "Donna says the name of that movie was *Magnificent Obsession*."

That Thanksgiving, Grandma played hostess for the entire family. Mom, Dad, and I dressed upstairs for the celebration. We'd just finished cleaning the basement, preparing it for the large, sit-down family dinner.

Mom and Dad finished dressing and went downstairs. As I ran a comb through my hair one last time, I heard muffled sounds rising up from the basement where my mother's family arrived for Thanksgiving dinner.

The laughter became louder as I walked downstairs through Grandma's apartment, then down the basement stairway. I peeked around the corner and pulled my sweater over my hips. With the onset of puberty, my figure was changing and I felt self-conscious entering the room.

"How's Diannie?" My grandmother's sister Dot smiled, looking up from a tray of olives she placed on the long table.

For a moment I hesitated. You're such a lovely person, I thought. After the death of her infant son, Auntie Dot was transformed into an individual of extraordinary beauty. She could soothe others' sorrow with her understanding and a willingness to share their burdens. Even though my grandmother's brothers and their wives had given a lot of time and support to her after the tragic auto accident, it was Auntie Dot's empathy and inner spiritual beauty that set her apart from everyone else.

Feeling more comfortable, I walked directly to her and gave her a kiss on the cheek. "Oh, I'm fine, Auntie Dot."

All the aunts bustled about, putting dinner on the large, triple-length table set up in the center of the room. Two huge stuffed golden-brown turkeys had a place of honor, one at each end of the table. Enticing aromas of the delicious meal filled the air. The men stood around the bar enjoying their holiday drinks. The talk and laughter grew louder and the basement appeared smaller than it was.

Finally, Grandma Verda called, "Dinner's on, come and get it!" All of us gathered around the large table with our own immediate families.

"Who's going to say the blessing?" Auntie Dot asked.

The room fell silent.

My father stood up. "Diane and I would like to sing the Lord's Prayer for you."

Surprised, I pushed my chair back, rose, and stood next to him. The clear tones of my young, second-soprano voice complemented Dad's harmonizing baritone. We finished the song and looked at one another with modest smiles and sat down reverently. The entire family seemed speechless, not knowing whether to say thank you or to applaud.

Uncle Ben, my grandmother's brother, spoke up. "That was beautiful." The others smiled and nodded in agreement.

Later, Dad and I recorded the Lord's Prayer on our Webcor recorder. I can still hear how beautiful we sounded together. After we finished our duet, Dad had turned to me, his eyes bright with a sparkle of delight. "A job well done," he said.

Heaven's gratitude came to me through this Thanksgiving memory. Christ imprinted His mark on my heart by revealing the spirit of His Sermon on the Mount.[5] Now He would send His angels that I might trust in Him.

---

[5] Refers to Matthew 6: 9-13, King James version. "After this manner therefore pray ye: Our Father which art in heaven, Hallowed be thy name."

CHAPTER TWELVE:
MY GUARDIAN ANGEL

Enlist angelic help through prayer

During the summer of 1989, I was finishing my college degree in therapeutic recreation and nearing the end of my fieldwork at a local hospital when I became seriously ill with a respiratory flu. My doctor ordered medication and bed rest for a couple of days and said to get up only when necessary.

I was in bed when I remembered that a charity agency truck would make a stop at our home to pick up used clothing. Alone in the house, I got up, trudged along the hallway, and made my way down the basement stairs. My breathing was heavy and my chest ached. I wondered if pneumonia felt this way.

Perspiration dripped off my forehead and down the front of my nightgown. I packed two small bags with clothing. I couldn't pack any more. It would have to be enough.

I picked up a clean, pink nightgown from the ironing board where I'd set it a few days before and headed for the stairway. Weak and breathless, I placed one hand on the banister and carefully climbed the stairs one at a time. "God, please let me make it to the kitchen. Just a few more steps." I reached the top of the stairs. "Please let me make it to the bedroom."

I had undiagnosed asthma and no idea how serious my condition was that afternoon. I entered the bedroom and laid my nightgown on the dresser. Falling onto the bed, I looked up at the ceiling in anger. "I'm going to die after all this work. I wanted to help so many people."

An unexplained feeling surged through me when I gave God permission to take me. A strong, dominant male voice answered me. "You're not going to die; you're going to help hundreds."

I sat up. Did I hear that? I must *really* be sick.

I changed into the fresh nightgown and lay back down on the bed, exhausted by the effort. Not more than two minutes passed when the telephone rang. I rolled slowly across the bed to answer it. "Hello," I said, my voice parched.

"Hi, Di." It was Rita. "I left you alone for a few days. How ya feeling?"

"Oh, Rita, I feel awful. I can't make it to the kitchen from the bedroom or the bedroom from the bathroom."

"Don't you think you should go to the hospital?" A tone of concern colored Rita's voice.

"Do you think so?"

"Yes," she insisted.

"But no one's home. Lloyd's at work and Valerie's at band rehearsal."

"Get dressed. I'll pick you up in twenty minutes." Rita hung up.

As I put the phone down, I looked upward and spoke aloud once more. "Boy, you work fast."

When we arrived at the hospital, I walked into the emergency room while Rita stayed in the outer hall at the information desk. Two nurses helped me onto a gurney and took my vital signs, then returned to the outer hall.

The next day Rita visited me on the cardiac unit and told me what they said.

"How did she get to the hospital?" one nurse asked.

"I brought her here myself," Rita told them. "I asked her if she could make it and she said yes."

"Another ten minutes and you would've had to call the paramedics for her," the second nurse said. "It doesn't look good. Her body is shutting down. Her blood pressure and heart rate are extremely low."

Rita was overwhelmed and asked if she could see me. "In a few minutes," they told her.

I lay on the gurney in a small curtained cubicle. A nurse in a light blue and white print smock and white slacks wiped my skin with rubbing alcohol and attached EKG sensors in the same spots. She asked me, "What's your address?"

"I know this sounds funny," I told her, "but I can't remember now." I felt unafraid, remembering only what my angel said in that stern voice: "You're not going to die. You're going to help hundreds."

I'd always thought angels might speak with sweet, angelic, and feminine voices. But my angel was a man. His voice wasn't familiar or unnatural. He had the strong voice of someone who was in control of the situation. I could hear it in his tone. It made me feel safe. Although I was now in my forties, I'd first felt his touch at the age of twelve.

I recalled a sweltering summer day in 1954 when my school girlfriends and I rode the bus to Chicago's Riis Park for a cool swim in the public pool. Each of us found an open window to sit near. With each stop and start of the bus, the heat of the steamy summer air blew back onto us. We told knock-knock jokes, laughed and talked about forming our own club and other adolescent girl interests all the way to the park.

When we went into our little dressing rooms, I watched each of my friends step out in their cute two-piece swimming suits and briefly stand under the shower. One of my girlfriends had always been slim. The other two girls were nicely proportioned for their size. Then there was me, a bit chubby, wearing a slimming one-piece suit with a skirt. I was embarrassed by my size and envied their smaller bodies, although they didn't seem to mind my overabundance.

Even though we'd all earned our Red Cross cards for beginner swimmers, we stayed in the shallow water most of the time. The pool area was packed. Kids circled the pool and milled around the ladders to the diving boards. Swimming was almost impossible. The four of us found a spot to lay our towels down and sun ourselves. Two of the girls swam to the other side of the pool. My other girlfriend and I swam and sunned alone. The second time I came out of the pool to lie in the sun, I started watching the kids jump off the high dive.

"I think I'll try the high dive," I said.

"You're crazy!" my girlfriend told me. "That board must be twenty feet off the ground."

"Oh, come on, I want to try it. Come with me!"

She shook her head. "I'll watch you."

As I jumped into the water, I called to her, "don't forget to watch for me, okay," and I swam off. I climbed out of the pool onto the hot concrete and stood in line with the others. The divers were doing flips, diving backwards, taking off feet first and head first. It didn't look hard to do. All of a sudden it was my turn.

I climbed the ladder and walked out to the very edge of the board. I looked back at the ladder, almost backing down, and saw the other divers watching me, waiting patiently. I thought, oh, what the heck, I'll go feet first. I jumped but lost a lot of air on the way down.

I hit the water and found myself standing on the bottom of the pool. I bent my knees to push up. Nothing happened. Not only did my body not rise to the top, it didn't even move from the bottom. I tried again. Still nothing. I realized then I was going to die. *Oh, God,* I prayed with an inward cry, *I can't get up. I'm going to die. Help me!*

I began seeing my life pass before me. I thought of Mom, Dad, and the accident. I remembered how my mother cared for her family at home after the accident and the pain they suffered from losing a loved one. Now I, their only child, was going to die!

Suddenly, I felt light as a feather as someone held me from behind, under the arms, and lifted. I saw a light as my body floated up toward the surface. I could hear kids laughing as I moved closer to the top of the water.

I broke through the surface, coughing, trying to get air back into my lungs. I reached for the side of the pool, wiped water out of my eyes with my free hand, and looked around to see who had pulled me up.

No one was there.

I looked over at the lifeguard's high white perch. He was still sitting there as he was when I first walked out onto the board. How could that be? Wasn't it the lifeguard who had saved me? Whoever had helped me was large and strong, but because he had been behind me, I hadn't seen him.

As I lifted myself out of the pool. I pretended to be pleased with my jump, never mentioning my experience with what I later realized was my guardian angel, Uriel.

My guardian angel protected me, guiding me toward a plan Christ wanted me to fulfill. I learned that serving as a vehicle for healing others would be part of this mission.

CHAPTER THIRTEEN:
THE SPIRITUAL HEART

Discover your life's mission

In the fall of 1989 I was employed by a local hospital as a Therapeutic Recreational Therapist. My experience as a nurse's aide and a caregiver for my mother helped me on the seventeen-bed, skilled-care unit of elderly patients that needed extended care before transferring to a rehabilitation unit.

I had worked there a year when asked to conduct the prayer service on Saturday. The assignment was a surprise and overwhelming because my religious education consisted only of attending and graduating from Lutheran parochial schools.

When Saturday arrived, I felt ready. The prayer service went well. After that, I continued conducting the services, never preparing ahead of time, relying instead on inner inspiration. I offered whatever seemed right for the people attending the services. I gave multi-denominational services, reading poems and prayers from the Catholic tradition, stories from the *Lutheran Digest,* and excerpts from the King James Version of the Bible. For music, I brought Tennessee Ernie Ford's hymns from my father's collection. *What a Friend We Have in Jesus, Jesus, Savior, Pilot Me,* and *His Eye Is on the Sparrow* played weekly in the recreation room.

After a few minutes, I got up and began laying my hands on each patient in the room as *His Eye Is on the Sparrow* played softly on the stereo. Spiritually guided from within, it seemed natural for me to do. As I touched the patients, heat traveled from my shoulders, down my arms, and into my hands.

I spoke to the patients. "Jesus is with you. I wish you well." They were visibly moved, and it was such an emotional experience for me that tears ran down my cheeks.

Not only did I feel the patients being blessed by God through me, I felt blessed while touching them. Many times I thought to myself, how ironic. Here I am giving a prayer service for people who aren't able to go to church for spiritual fulfillment because of their illness. On the other hand, I left church because I wasn't fulfilled. Through leading prayer services for others, Christ had given me a new way to serve, through spiritual healing.

I made daily visits to the patients' rooms to ask them whether they preferred to do an individual activity or join the other patients for a group activity. One day I entered a patient's room and found her sitting in a wheelchair with her head down. Her long gray hair appeared to be uncombed.

"Good morning," I said pleasantly. As I spoke, she looked up. "Would you like me to give you a manicure this morning?"

"Why bother? There's nothing to live for." Her face appeared slack and depressed.

When you work with the elderly, you hear that response often. I looked at her for a moment. "You're not ready to go yet. If you were, you wouldn't be here."

"Are you a social worker?"

"No, I'm not a social worker. Forty years ago I might have been considered one, but the job field expanded. As it grew, so did the paperwork. I wanted a closer relationship with patients, more like being a family member. People are too busy getting ahead in the world. They don't have the time to visit. Hospitals hire people like me to help people like you," I told her.

"My daughter is divorced. She has to work full time, and she can't visit me as often as she'd like."

"You're lucky to have a daughter who cares to visit you. Many of my patients have no one. Sadly, some of my patients' families don't care enough to visit them at all. People have forgotten what's important in life, that caring for others from the heart can heal or save lives. And that helping others creates a spiritual reward. "

"Have you ever been rewarded for what you do here?" Her eyes glittered with a new spark.

"Every day I'm rewarded by a smile, a thank you, or a kind word. But the spiritual reward I'm talking about isn't the same. First of all," I said, "you can't think of doing something good for someone and expecting a reward for it. It's not from your heart then; that's greed. What I do won't work that way. You expect nothing for what you do. Heaven knows what you need or desire and will make it possible for you to have it."

She nodded with a knowing look.

"I've got an idea! I'm giving a Valentine social in the recreation room this afternoon, and I could use some help. Would you like to be my assistant?"

"Oh, I don't know . . . what could I do?"

"Just socialize with everyone. Call it a labor of love. I only have three patients alert enough to enjoy the social and one of my patients is blind. Remember, if you help, you have to do it with a joyful heart. I'll come back later this afternoon and see if you'd like to assist me or if you'd rather join the other patients."

"Okay, we'll see."

"Now let me tell you a true story about my Angel Uriel and how he saved my life when I was a child, and spoke to me again nearly forty years later." I told her about the incident at the swimming pool and about the voice affirming I would recover when I was at death's door.

She listened intently. "How did you come by that angel name?"

"Thirty years ago I read a book on angels. The name Uriel has something to do with art and music. Since I'm interested in both, you can see why I chose that name." I pointed to the angel pin I wore daily on the shoulder of a brightly colored blouse. "Do you see this pin? My friend Barbara Allen sent it to me after my angel spoke to me the second time. She wanted me to have it because, in her words, I walked with angels."

"You're spiritual, aren't you?"

95

"Uh . . . I guess I am," I stammered. "Why?"

"What I've read about spiritual people is that their life on earth isn't easy. Their whole being seems to be directed toward inspiring others and saving the world in some way." She paused a moment, trying to find the right words. "People see a sparkle of light in the spiritual, and some are repelled by the light. These people have a tendency to destroy what they don't understand and they hurt those beautiful creatures of God. They have for centuries. You see, some never knew that good and evil were warring against each other for control of their hearts." She hesitated again, peering at me. "Now tell me, isn't that the way it is for you? Aren't you constantly hurt by the insults of other people? You know, people with hidden problems and sometimes even strangers?"

"How did you know that?"

Again, she looked at me closely. "You were chosen."

"Chosen?"

"There's a reason why you lived. A purpose," she told me. Her face brightened, and her depression lifted as she candidly shared her wisdom.

I smiled back at her. "Now how about those nails? I want to make you feel beautiful while you're waiting."

All day I thought of her words: You were chosen. There's a reason why you lived, a purpose. . . The reason was here at the hospital. What better way to help so many people? My greatest ability was hidden. I was able to sense danger through my heightened intuition. When I was in a room with someone, I could sense illness, and I often alerted the medical staff to a patient's worsening condition and prevented a tragic event. That was a gratifying experience. I loved being in a position to help all of them. I had saved eight, maybe ten lives. Perhaps more. My thoughts turned back to the first person I'd saved, before I started working at the hospital.

"Di, I'd like to give your mother a surprise birthday party next month," Rita said, excited about her plans.

"That's a great idea, but don't you think it's too soon?"

"No, I don't. Aunt Donna needs a little cheering up. Just because your father died three weeks ago doesn't mean the whole world has stopped turning," she said.

"It did stop for her, Rita, but you're right. She needs to feel we all care. Thanks for thinking of her," I conceded.

Family and friends gathered at Rita's home for Mom's surprise celebration the first week of March. Warm hellos peppered the initial surprise, followed by the usual loud conversation coupled with genuine laughter.

My cousins and aunts placed their favorite casseroles, fresh salads, and Jell-O molds on the large circular table. Rita arranged the Italian beef next to the crusty French rolls. "Dinner's ready," she announced, and we formed a line at the buffet style meal to help ourselves.

As I walked toward the bar where I'd previously been sitting with Lloyd, I noticed Mom between Valerie and Aunt Mary on the couch and smiled as I passed them.

I'd just sat down with my plate when Rita came up and grabbed my arm, her voice tinged with urgency. "Di, I think you'd better look at your mother."

"Huh?"

She pulled me off the barstool insistently. "Something's wrong with your mother."

Mom's arms were in midair and her eyes penetrated mine. She couldn't talk. Taking her by her raised hands, I brought her to a standing position. She wasn't breathing. I turned her around and hit the upper part of her back a few times. Nothing. Standing behind her, I placed my arms around her and interlocked my fingers into one large fist. I pushed my fist into her abdomen sharply, twice. Up came a large chunk of sandwich. She coughed for a moment, then breathed for the first time in minutes.

Four years later, our fire department paramedics came into Mom's restaurant to place a sign behind the cash register. I was busy with customers, and Mom phoned an order for food supplies in the storeroom. Later, during the afternoon lull, I read the sign for the first time. There, in large red lettering were instructions for performing something called the Heimlich maneuver.

"What!" I exclaimed, in total shock. Two customers turned toward me. "Why that's the technique I used on my mother four years ago at her surprise birthday party. I had no idea what it was."

"Sounds like that was some surprising birthday gift you gave your mother," one of them said. "Her life!"

"I guess I did save her. Yes, I saved her." I felt proud.

From behind the soda fountain, my mother's voice sounded loud and clear: "I bet you're sorry!"

One day, late in the spring of 1976, I was helping Mom at the restaurant. "Mom, the delivery man is here with supplies."

I grabbed a box of hamburgers thawing on the butcher-block kitchen table, then hurried past her to the grill, wearing our summer uniform, white bell-bottom slacks and a soft pink and white polyester blouse. I placed the hamburgers into the cooler behind the counter.

"Diane, can you take some orders?"

I looked up to see Mom's steadfast waitress, Sophie. "I need an order of potatoes with crisp bacon on the side. I'll make the eggs—they're very particular people—and you can make a BLT, light on the mayonnaise."

When there was a lull, Nancy, mom's cashier, signaled me, nodding in the direction of the first table. "Diane, is something wrong with that man's sandwich? He's not eating it."

I glanced over and saw Bob from the nearby Mercedes Benz dealership. I walked over and smiled. "Don't you like your sandwich, Bob?"

He looked up at me. "I guess I'm not very hungry. I really don't feel like eating today." His voice seemed softer than usual.

"Would you like something else?"

"No, no, I can't even eat this. Thanks."

I went back to the register, and still watching Bob, spoke to the cashier. "He doesn't feel like eating, Nancy."

"Well, at least it's not the food, then."

Startled, I looked at Nancy, then at Bob again. "No, it's not the sandwich. Listen, Nancy, it's noon, and I have to go back on the grill. Will you do a favor for me? Bob's sick. Call the paramedics." I walked back to Bob's table. "We're calling the paramedics for you."

He searched my face for a moment. "No, no, that's okay. I'm not that sick," he protested weakly.

Two months later, Bob came into the restaurant one afternoon and stood beside the counter. "Did you miss me?"

"Yes," I exclaimed. "How are you?"

"Remember when you had paramedics come for me during that busy lunch hour? Well, Diane, I've been in the hospital all this time. You saved me from a massive heart attack." With a broad smile, Bob leaned over the counter and patted my upper arm. "I just stopped in to say thank you."

When he touched me, I thought I felt a slight twinge. "I didn't do anything. I'm just glad you're all right."

"Oh, I know you did more than that, Diane." He paused, and then asked, "What can I do for you?"

"Nothing, I don't want anything."

"There must be something."

I reflected on his words. "There is something you might help me with. My husband remodeled our kitchen and we chose cabinets in dark fruitwood. Do you know where we can purchase a hand-made wooden clock to match the cabinets?"

"I believe I do. Have you ever heard of the Amana Colonies in Iowa?"

I hesitated for a moment. "Yes, we discussed the Mennonites in high school. I didn't know you could visit the Amana Colonies."

Bob nodded. "The colonies are villages with quaint little shops. They sell all kinds of different items; many are handmade. They have wines, breads, furniture, and a restaurant with wonderful old-style German food. My wife and I went there last year on a weekend trip. Joan bought a handcrafted walnut cabinet in one of the shops. Plain, but beautiful. Their work has exceptional craftsmanship."

"I'll tell my husband about taking a trip there. Thanks for telling me about them."

One afternoon a few weeks later, Bob came into the restaurant for lunch. I was busy on the grill with the waitresses' orders and didn't get a chance to talk to him. After that, I never saw Bob again, and wondered if he was still alive. It touched my heart when he'd stopped in to say thank you and I'd always remember the empathy in his words.

These incidents showed me that a plan for my life had manifested. Yet one day I'd doubt Valerie's spiritual experience with her own angel.

CHAPTER FOURTEEN:
AN ANGEL AMONG US

Angels arrive at our hour of need

In 1991, Valerie met and married a young man named Mark. Two years later, Lloyd and I became grandparents to a beautiful baby boy, Luke Carrington. On the day of Luke's birth, Valerie telephoned me. It was her first day off work from her secretarial position at a local company where Mark was also employed. "I woke up early this morning and cleaned out all the kitchen cabinets and all the closets," she told me.

"I remember when *you* were ready to be born. Everything had to be just so. I even painted the windowsill in the kitchen. With all the cleaning you're doing, Val, it sounds like you're ready to give birth."

"I know, Mom, they call it nesting."

"Have you had any contractions? You know, like menstrual cramps?"

"No, nothing. But I'm tired. I think I'll hang up and lie down for awhile."

It was after three in the afternoon when Valerie phoned again. She told me that after her nap, the contractions had finally begun. She'd called Mark home from work, and they planned to leave for the doctor's office.

After the call, I looked at the kitchen calendar hanging inside the pantry. If the baby were born that evening, April 5, it would arrive on the eve of Passover.

On the first Passover, the angel of the Lord passed over the homes of the Hebrews, and if they followed God's command through Moses, the lives of the firstborn sons were spared.[6] I wondered if Valerie realized what day it was. I poured myself a glass of iced tea and took a sip. Did she remember the Bible stories she'd heard at the little Lutheran grammar school she attended? Both the Old and New Testaments of the Bible were diligently taught there.

Only last month, Valerie shared her and Mark's plans for the baby's christening. The baby would be baptized a Protestant at a Lutheran church near their home. They had chosen Mark's boyhood friend Keith, from the Jewish faith, and Valerie's childhood friend Sally, brought up Catholic, to be the new baby's godfather and godmother. Even I was a little surprised at their choice of godparents, but as I thought about it, I found a special significance in the beauty of their plan. The Old and New Testaments of the Bible would unite for one child's baptism.

After five in the evening, while I finished the dinner dishes, I noticed myself pacing across the kitchen. I arched my shoulders, then rubbed my lower back, wishing the ache would go away. I felt uneasy.

"Lloyd, I think we'd better go to the hospital. I called a little while ago to see if Valerie had registered yet, but the operator put me through to the birthing room. I let the phone ring a few times, but there wasn't any answer. She must be in the delivery room."

"They'll call when the baby's born, Diane," Lloyd answered matter-of-factly.

"Yes, but if anything goes wrong, I want to be there, Lloyd."

"Okay. All right, we'll go."

When we arrived at the hospital, the door to Valerie's room was closed. Through it, we heard muffled voices. We hesitated, turning back to the nurse's station.

"Yes, you can go into the birthing room. They're in there. They had a boy!"

---

[6] Exodus 12: 13, King James version. "And the blood shall be to you for a token upon the houses where ye are. And when I see the blood, I will pass over you and the plague shall not be upon you to destroy you, when I smite the land of Egypt."

When Lloyd and I entered the room, Mark stood next to the hospital bed, holding our new grandson in a white receiving blanket. Valerie reclined in what appeared to be a large, overstuffed lounger. The fulfillment of motherhood graced her, and she smiled endlessly. Mark greeted us, and we both peered into the baby's precious little face.

"Oh, he's so tiny, I said, touching his fingers.

Lloyd glanced up at Valerie. "A little seed from our Pumpkin," he said, referring to the pet name he'd given Valerie when she was born.

"Oh, Mom and Dad," she said, "Keith and Amy called just before you came in. They're celebrating the eve of Passover tonight at their home. Isn't that something? Luke, the firstborn, coming into the world at Passover?"

I nodded proudly. She remembered the biblical story as I thought she might.

"Do you want to hold him?" Mark asked.

I nearly jumped for joy. "Of course." He placed the baby in my arms. "Luke," I said to the tiny baby . . . "Why, Valerie, he turned his head and looked at me when I said his name. I've never seen a newborn do that!"

Valerie bubbled with excitement. "I didn't know he'd been completely born until the doctor placed him on my tummy. Luke lifted his head and looked directly into my face. If having a baby is this easy, I want five! This afternoon at the doctor's office, I had slight contractions. The doctor told me I was already dilated six centimeters. He said I was in hard labor. When we got here, they put me into this birthing room for labor and delivery. They wouldn't tell me anything. It was all so fast! My back hurt for about two minutes."

I recalled my backache in the kitchen about the same time.

"The nurse began rubbing my back, but the pain disappeared. Luke never hurt me, being born. I gave three pushes, and do you know, on the first push, someone called me on the phone? Can you imagine that?"

I gave her a sheepish grin. "It was me," I admitted. "The operator connected me directly to the birthing room."

As time passed, Luke's hair became light brown with a reddish cast. His dark blue eyes were large and bright. He smiled often, and

103

his excited, happy reaction to seeing us made us eager to touch or hold him. Joy filled our hearts every time he was near. The summer of 1993 was the happiest season our family had experienced in a long time.

One Sunday afternoon Lloyd and I stopped at Valerie's home. The previous fall, Valerie and Mark purchased a small, three-bedroom ranch house in a well-established neighborhood. Trees lined the streets and although the houses were similar, carefully chosen siding or paint gave each one an individual look.

Valerie busied herself making dinner. When it came time for Luke's feeding, Valerie picked up the baby from his little seat on the table and gave him to me while she warmed his bottle in the microwave. Every time I looked into his face as he lay cradled in my arms, I'd see one of our relatives. Today I thought he looked like my mother.

I smiled at Valerie as she worked around the room. "I hate to say this, but Luke's even better looking than you when you were a baby."

Valerie turned and looked at me with an "I know" expression on her face. She seemed proud of the fact that she had a beautiful little boy. There didn't seem to be any other words to say except that Luke was more wonderful than any of us had expected.

As the weeks went by, Luke became charming, sweet, and loving. He had an irresistible little laugh that attracted people. Everyone wanted to be close to him. He loved animals, beautiful music, his mother's singing, his father's humor, and all the love and attention he could charm from everyone.

In late August, Mark and Valerie invited Lloyd and me to their home for dinner. When we entered their country-style kitchen, Luke sat in his little blue infant seat on the kitchen floor.

"Hi, little guy." Lloyd bent down to greet Luke. He smiled back under his pacifier, which began moving rapidly as he noticed Lloyd.

I leaned forward. "Hi, Lukie." Luke turned his head toward me and kept smiling.

"Mark will be in from the grill in a minute. The roast is almost done." Valerie glanced at her husband through the patio door while she bustled around the kitchen, warming Luke's bottle and making a salad.

Lloyd brushed past me, heading for the patio. "I'll see what Mark's up to."

"Is there anything you want me to do, Val?" I asked.

"Do you want to give Luke his bottle before I put him to bed? You and dad missed his bath time again."

"Sure, I'd like that."

Val handed me the bottle, removed Luke from the infant seat and placed him on my lap.

Cradled in my arms, I gave him the bottle. Luke's hands cupped it with tiny fingers; three curled around one of mine.

"How's Grandma's sweetheart?" I asked. Luke's eyes danced with pleasure.

Lloyd opened the patio door. "Roast's done," Mark announced, placing the meat on the kitchen counter cutting board.

Luke turned his head, smiling at the sound of his father's voice. A milk ring surrounded his mouth when the nipple popped out.

"Look at Luke, he smiled when he heard Mark," I said.

"It's just gas, Mom." Val grinned.

I smiled at the joke. I told Val the same thing when she brought newborn Luke home from the hospital. "Is there anything else you want us to do, Val?"

"Oh, just enjoy the baby," she exclaimed. "You can put him down for the night before we sit down for dinner."

I rose from the chair with the sleepy baby in my arms. "Grandma will sing you to sleep with a little song, Lukie." I started to hum the old nursery tune *Hush Little Baby, Don't You Cry.*

"Oh, no!" Mark and Val said in unison. "Luke hates that song."

I tossed my head back, lowered my eyelids, and drew my lips together in a puckish sneer. Turning toward the hallway, I blurted at them in a high society accent. "Well!"

We'd just finished dessert when Valerie said shyly, "I met my angel today."

Lloyd smiled. Mark didn't know what to say. Laughing, I said, "Oh, Val, you're reading too many of those angel books." I knew Valerie was impressionable and thought that maybe her reading had ignited her imagination.

Mark kidded with her. "It was some dirty old man trying to pick her up."

Valerie insisted it was her angel. "Yesterday, when I went to the supermarket, I felt depressed because a man at work said I looked fat in my slacks. I know I haven't lost all my pregnancy weight, but wasn't that an awful thing to say to a woman who just had a baby a few months ago?"

I nodded. "Yes, that was thoughtless."

"Well, I was looking at picture frames when out of the corner of my eye I noticed a man coming down the aisle, smiling. He walked past me, then turned around and came back. He looked directly at me. 'You're just a beautiful girl. You have beautiful eyes and beautiful hair.' As I looked at him, I was in awe. There was something so peaceful about him." Valerie's voice softened. "He wore white and powder blue. I noticed perfect teeth with his huge smile. I remember him saying, 'I thought you needed to hear that.' And he walked away. I kept thinking, oh, my God. It was my angel."

Her conclusion was hard for us to accept, and we made light of it. Valerie insisted, "I swear, I met my angel."

A couple of weeks later, my phone rang and Valerie said, "Mom, I saw him again."

"Who did you see?"

"My angel."

I hesitated. "Oh, your angel."

"I was in a different grocery store, near the dairy section. Luke was in the little seat in the cart. All of a sudden, there was the same man with his hands on the cart looking at Luke. He looked at me and said, 'What a beautiful baby.' His voice had such a calming effect on me."

No one I knew ever had such an experience. Seeing an angel? In a grocery store? Two separate stores, same man? Logically dismissing her experience as the effect of an overactive imagination, I interrupted her. "You let some strange man get that close to Luke? The world is full of people who steal children."

Valerie was upset with my reaction to her story. "Mom, it wasn't like that. I wasn't afraid of him hurting the baby."

"What did he look like?"

"He looked the same, but he wasn't wearing the same clothes as the last time. His cheeks were rosy, and he had that perfect smile."

"How old would you say he was?"

"Oh, I don't know. Daddy's age, fifty-four or so. As he walked away he was still smiling at me. His smile seemed to say, 'You know who I am.' The same feeling came over me the last time. I met my angel, Mom."

Soon I understood why Valerie needed such a strong experience in meeting her angel. She was closer to a truth none of us wanted to believe, a truth that only God in His infinite wisdom controlled.

Chapter Fifteen: The Cherub

Recognize Earth angels

In October, Valerie asked if Lloyd and I would take care of Luke for a few hours while she and Mark attended a party held in a restaurant near our home. "Sure, Val," I told her, "bring him over. We'll be home."

After Luke was born, Lloyd set up a small white crib in our dining room for those special occasions when the baby came to visit. The little crib sat next to the wall dividing the kitchen and the dining room. In the center of the room sat our small octagonal marble table with three powder blue chairs around it. Over the table was a four-tiered crystal chandelier. Every time I went into the dining room to change Luke or put him to sleep, I'd turn on the chandelier, then dim or brighten the lights so the prisms would glimmer. It was splendid to look at. I stood in the doorway admiring the scene, wondering if Heaven had crystal chandeliers.

Tonight seemed no different from any other night we cared for Luke. Val told us Luke had an earache earlier and handed me a bottle of medicine, but he seemed fine now. After Mark and Val left, Lloyd played with him a while in the family room.

"Hi, little guy." Lloyd spoke softly, and Luke smiled and cooed at him. "Give me a kiss, fella." Not knowing how to pucker, Luke opened his mouth, leaned toward Lloyd and pressed his face to his grandfather's. I couldn't help feeling a bit jealous watching them while

I fixed Luke's bottle for his feeding, but when the bottle was warm, Lloyd put the baby into my arms.

As I fed him, I noticed his little back was ramrod straight. He sat gazing around the room and softly whimpered one time; I wondered if he missed his parents. After he drank only an ounce of formula, he didn't seem to want any more. I carried him into the dining room and lay him in the little crib on his back, so he could see the chandelier. While I changed his diaper, he cooed and looked into my face.

"There, sweetheart, all done." I smiled and played with the chandelier's dimmer switch for a few seconds. The prisms changed colors from blue hues to yellow. Then I dimmed the lights until the warm glow of amber appeared.

Luke studied the changing colors, his arms bouncing up and down on the mattress. He smiled, then cooed, and up went his arms again. I turned the dimmer switch up enough to let the blue and yellow hues appear.

Luke feels safe now, I thought. He's remembering what Heaven is like, with all its gleaming colors.

Valerie phoned to check on Luke. "He's fine, such a good baby," I told her. "He loves to stay with Grandma and Grandpa. He's never any trouble."

"We'll be home in a couple of hours, Mom."

"Okay, honey, see you then." I hung up and peeked into the dining room. Luke was sleeping sweetly.

A couple of hours later, Val and Mark came to the door, quietly entered the house and went to look at Luke. "He's sleeping on his back." Val looked up at Mark, surprised. "He hates sleeping on his back."

"He sleeps on his back for Grandma," I whispered, trying to reassure her.

Just then, Luke became aware of his parents. Soon, all that could be heard were the soft sounds of baby talk from Mark and Valerie and cooing from Luke. How happy the three of them sounded. Mark and I smiled contentedly at each other as he passed me in the kitchen on his way to join Lloyd, who watched television in the living room.

Valerie entered the kitchen carrying Luke on her hip. The baby smiled, his bright eyes still looking with surprise at the world around him. "He's trying to crawl, Mom. He almost has it figured out, but his feet get crossed. Then he rocks back and forth. Would you like to see?"

I smiled at the thought. "I'd love to."

We joined Mark and Lloyd in the family room. Val sat on the couch and placed Luke on the floor in front of her.

"Mom, see? He tries to crawl, then seems afraid to go any farther."

I knelt on the floor beside Luke and crouched into a crawling position. "Grandma will show you how to crawl, Lukie. You can do it." I did an exaggerated crawl as Lloyd, Mark and Valerie watched us. "Come on, Luke, you can do it." Luke's eyes followed me as I crawled around on the beige carpet.

For one brief moment, Luke threw his head back like a pony and looked at me out of the corner of his enormous bright blue eyes. He opened his mouth in a silent laugh.

I thought, My God, if he had wings, he'd look like a cherub.

His celestial appearance filled me with joy. Rising from my hands and knees, I walked over, picked him up, and gently carried him to the other side of the couch. We were in full view of Mark, Valerie, and Lloyd, but I was completely focused on Luke. This was our moment.

I lay down on the floor with him on my stomach, but noticed we were so close to the coffee table's glass top that I became afraid he might bump it and hurt himself. I placed him on the floor as I sat up, but the movement was apparently too fast for him and he started crying.

Mark, who sat on the loveseat directly across from us, scowled. "What are you . . . stupid?" He stopped the sentence too late.

My heart sank. Had that come from Mark? Such an out-of-character remark. Too hurt to reply, I turned, picked Luke up, and handed him to his mother.

"Mom, Luke's ears hurt," Val tried to explain. "We should get going."

I rose. My mouth felt dry and I couldn't bring myself to look at Mark's face as they gathered Luke's belongings.

"Well, thanks for watching the baby for us." With the diaper bag in one hand and Luke's walker in the other, Valerie gave us both a kiss and walked toward the garage. "Talk to you tomorrow, Mom. Bye, Dad."

My heart still ached. "Bye, honey."

Lloyd followed her outside, helping her load their black Blazer. Mark came into the family room holding Luke in his car seat. I looked directly at Luke, his large blue eyes penetrating mine. He smiled at me. I touched his little legs. You're always smiling, baby, but are you all right? Unbidden, another thought came. Is something wrong with your brain, sweetheart?

At that moment, I heard a deep voice. "Grandma, he didn't mean it." The voice called me Grandma, but unmistakably, it was my angel's voice. I asked myself, why am I hearing my angel's voice at this particular moment?

I looked up at Mark. It seemed obvious he hadn't heard anything. I gave him a brief smile and lowered my eyes to Luke. "Bye, sweetheart. Come back to Grandma's and Grandpa's again."

I followed Mark and the baby to the driveway. He fastened Luke's little car seat into the Blazer. I peered through the window and waved. "Bye, Lukie, we love you, honey." Turning his face toward me, he smiled again.

We watched the car pull into the street, unaware this would be the last time our grandson would come and see his Grandpa and Grandma. As Lloyd and I turned and went back into the house, I knew something supernatural had taken place. I was afraid to admit it to myself. My angel intervened just as I'd touched Luke, to interrupt my premonition, directing the focus to my hurt feelings. I'd sensed a physical illness in his future that my angel wanted to hide from me. In a few weeks, I'd understand the spiritual blockage of my ability to receive information through my sense of touch.

Soon I'd realize why Heaven had given me signs from God, preparing me for what was to come.

Chapter Sixteen:
A Gift from Luke

Find love and everlasting life in family ties

Two weeks later, Valerie called and told me Luke's earache had worsened. She and Mark took him to the doctor the night before and scheduled another appointment the next afternoon. As Valerie lay on the sofa holding Luke on her stomach, she talked to me on the phone. When we mentioned his illness, he cried out. The sound frightened me—a weak, short, one-breath cry.

"Valerie, he sounds so sick." I tried conveying my deep concern without scaring her.

"We were at the doctor's last night," she explained, "and Luke sat up, cooed, and drank some Pedialyte mineral water. We're scheduled to go back again at one."

I felt somewhat reassured she was taking Luke to the doctor. He had treated Luke with antibiotics for his earache and fever. "Call if you need me, honey," I told her, and went upstairs to finish getting ready for work.

While I dressed, thoughts of Luke kept crossing my mind. Every morning I asked my angel Uriel to protect our home and our loved ones. I asked him to say hello to my mom, dad, and grandparents, and to tell Jesus that I love Him.

The clock had just struck ten when I opened the door to the garage. Keys in hand, I turned back and yelled into the house

"Uriel, Luke is sick."

I sensed movement. Wings touched my shoulders as a large figure rose behind me. With the speed of light, Uriel was gone. I felt assured my angel had heard my call for help, but I lacked a sense of urgency. I left for work not fully understanding this forewarning of the coming tragedy.

Later that morning, Valerie phoned me from a hospital near their home. Luke stopped breathing in her arms on the way to the hospital.

"Mom, I'm in the hospital's emergency room with Luke."

My heart dropped. "Do they know what's wrong with him?"

"They haven't said anything. Only that they were transferring him by helicopter to another facility with a more advanced medical team and equipment."

"I'll call your Dad, so he can meet us at the hospital."

"Don't come here. Go to the emergency room at the other hospital. They already know you're coming and will take you to the children's intensive care unit. We'll meet you upstairs in the waiting room."

"Okay, honey." I heard the sound of an engine running as we spoke. I pressed the phone closer to my ear to hear her.

"Mom, I have to hang up. They're loading Luke onto the emergency helicopter. He'll be flying through the air any second now. Both Mark and I want to be at the launching pad to see him off. Bye."

Lloyd arrived at the hospital a few minutes before me. As he parked the car, he watched the helicopter land and the medical team rush Luke into the emergency entrance. After they entered the hospital, Lloyd followed.

When I arrived at the emergency unit, my knees felt weak. I walked up to the information desk. "Miss, could you direct me to the children's intensive care unit?"

Before the receptionist could answer, the hospital chaplain came to my side and interrupted. "Are you Luke's grandmother?"

I looked at him, but the sound of his voice seemed not to come from him. Dazed, I answered, "Yes."

"We've been waiting for you. Would you like a wheelchair?"

"No, I'm fine."

The chaplain sensed confusion and gently asked again. "Are you sure? I'm going upstairs. I'll take you. It's no trouble."

Maybe he's right, I thought, my knees do feel weak. What if I fall? What kind of support could I give then?

"Okay," I told him.

When we reached the Children's Intensive Care unit, I left the wheelchair and walked shakily to the waiting room. It started filling with family and friends. The nurses took Valerie and Mark into a private office and a social worker told them about Luke's grave condition. When they returned to the waiting room, Valerie went to a side table, drew a couple of tissues from a holder, and faced the gathered group.

"Luke has bacterial meningitis. They're doing everything possible to help him. We'll know more in a few hours. Mark and I will stay in his room awhile. Each of you can take a turn to be with him," Valerie told us, blotting her eyes.

One by one, and two by two, we went into Luke's room. The heavily coated equipment cords lay skewed beneath our feet. We found it impossible to get closer than the equipment and stood side-by-side with it, hoping somehow the machines and the energy of our love would be strong enough to save him.

After several hours, Valerie made another announcement in the waiting room. "We're waiting for the brain scan to come back from the lab. It won't be ready until tomorrow. If you'd like to go home, we'll call when we hear something. Mark and I will stay here tonight."

The next morning, Valerie called us at home. The test had come back from the laboratory.

"Mom, could you and Dad come back to the hospital? They're taking Luke off life-support at 11:30 a.m." Her voice trailed off into a deafening silence.

I didn't want to believe what I'd heard. "There's nothing more they can do?" I cried.

"No."

"We'll be there." I prepared for Luke's death in a daze of disbelief.

Late that morning, Luke's parents, grandparents, godparents, family members, and friends gathered to witness the passing of Luke's earthly life. We stood around Valerie, who sat in a rocking chair cradling him. Mark stood against the wall to the right of them with a look of desperate confusion on his face. Saddened, his parents stood to his right. I stood behind Valerie and placed my hands on her shoulders. Lloyd stood behind me. The pastor who had baptized Luke spoke to us about a heavenly gathering and said each of us would see him again. The Reverend finished his speech, closing with the Lord's Prayer.

Those closest to the door started leaving the room. As if on cue, Valerie, still cradling Luke, looked up at Mark with unbridled joy. "Mark, quick, call the nurse, he moved. Luke's coming back to life!"

The nurse unplugging the life support system from the far side of the room had gone unnoticed. As she untwisted the life support cord, she turned to Valerie with great empathy. "The cord accidentally became twisted and interrupted the flow of oxygen. When this happens, the body naturally contracts and starts moving."

Valerie rose with Luke in her arms and placed him on the hospital bed. Depleted of all hope, she slumped back down into the rocker. Mark stood next to her, silent. They waited for the involuntary movements to stop.

Lloyd and I ate in silence that first night. Tears flowed nonstop and the meal I'd prepared was tasteless.

Lloyd was inconsolable. "He died because of the way I am. Why didn't God take me instead of that tiny baby? I'm the one who's sick." Lloyd wept, referring to his diabetes.

"I wish He had taken me," I blurted, brushing away tears.

As the days passed, our devastation continued. The pain of losing Luke was unbearable. Neither Lloyd nor I wanted Valerie to suffer the pain of losing him. We'd rather have died in his place. It was impossible for any of us to understand the baby's death. Luke was only six and half months old. He had wonderful, caring parents who loved him. His grandparents, family, and friends adored him. Luke had everything.

Why?

The day after Luke's burial, Lloyd and I went over to Mark and Valerie's home. They opened their door together. Mark had just returned from taking a friend to the airport. His friend had flown in from Arizona for Luke's funeral.

Lloyd and I carried a couple of grocery bags into the kitchen. As we set them on the table, I asked, "Valerie, is there anything you want us to do?"

Lloyd repeated my question. "Do you need anything, Valerie?"

"No, nothing," she replied dolefully.

Mark took our winter coats and hung them in the hallway closet as Lloyd and I sat down at the kitchen table.

Valerie leaned forward. She had no makeup on, and her eyes were puffy and swollen from crying. "This morning Mark and his friend Mike were sitting here at the table. I'd gone into the bedroom to get dressed, when Mark called to me from the kitchen, 'Val, Val, look what Luke sent us!' I rushed into the kitchen. Mark and Mike stood in front of the patio doors. Mark moved aside and said to me, 'Look at this.' I gazed into the yard. The patio and the entire backyard were covered with mallard ducks! There weren't one or two ducks, but an entire flock of fifteen or more."

Mark joined us at the table, and Valerie continued. "I slid the patio door open a little, afraid the ducks would fly away. Mark handed me some popcorn he'd taken from the cabinet. The three of us edged out onto the patio, and the ducks didn't flinch. They waddled around the patio, unafraid of us."

Lloyd and I sat there, stunned. How very unusual, a flock of ducks setting down in their small backyard, one of the many small fenced yards behind the homes on the block.

Tears welled up in Mark and Valerie's eyes. "Remember how Luke loved the ducks and geese at the zoo, Mark?" Val asked, her voice wavering with emotion.

Only a few weeks before, Mark and Valerie had shown us the videotape they'd taken at the zoo where they introduced Luke to his first duck. How excited he'd been, pointing at the ducks, his mouth open with glee.

A pained look crossed Mark's face. Val placed her hand on his arm. He rose from the table and went to the living room. Lloyd followed.

Valerie and I were silent for a few moments. "Mom, what are you thinking about?"

"That afternoon we went to Rita's house. Remember?"

Valerie nodded.

I recalled the day. "Rita, Mark, you, and your dad carried Luke out to the edge of the golf course. Rita pointed at the geese circling in the sky and they flew down. She threw pieces of bread to them on the lawn. You and Mark were in awe of the geese and so was Luke. . . You know, I stood inside the kitchen behind those glass doors, watching and wondering if a baby could remember those geese flying and landing and feeding." I looked at Valerie. "Mark's right," I said. "It's a gift from Luke!"

This time, I knew it was true.

None of us completely realized the importance of the mallard duck blessing at the time. Luke came to say goodbye in a way Valerie and Mark understood. Heaven sent ducks as a remembrance of Luke's life. God's love had manifested as a natural wonder, a message forever embedded in their hearts.

"Mom, there's something else. Come into Luke's bedroom."

I followed Valerie down the hallway, and she opened the closed door of the nursery. She walked over to the crib, picked up Luke's blanket and handed it to me. "Smell this, Mom. Does it smell like flowers?"

I put the blanket up to my face. I'm sure a look of surprise brightened it. "Not just flowers, Valerie. I smell roses! I haven't smelled roses on fabric since Grandma Verda died thirty years ago."

"Then I'm not going crazy?"

"No, honey, you're not going crazy. I smell them, too. It means everything is okay. Luke's at peace."

With a heart full of tenderness, I glanced at my daughter and spoke to her inwardly. *I love you, Val.*

"I asked Mark if he smelled flowers," Valerie continued. "He said yes, but he thought the blanket had been at the funeral home. But Mom, we didn't use this blanket. We took Luke's white christening blanket with the featherstitch that you and Dad gave him."

I looked at the folded christening blanket on the rocking chair in the corner of the nursery. It was the same rocker Valerie's great-great grandmother used to tell tales, recite poems, and sing to her grandchildren, then her great-grandchildren. The same chair Valerie rocked Luke in while she sang him to sleep. In a family of firstborn daughters, Luke had been the only firstborn son in over 120 years.

I remembered Valerie saying she rocked Luke to sleep while she sang Rod Stewart's ballad, *Have I Told You Lately?*

"Val, he's with the generations," I said, looking into her eyes.

Christ helped heal us through our five senses, deepening our relationship with Him. Gifts from Heaven and our love for Him furthered my family's healing.

Chapter Seventeen: Heartstrings from Heaven

Listen for heavenly music

It was unusual for me to wake up before the alarm went off. One morning soon after Luke's death, I tried falling back to sleep for those last few minutes. But I kept thinking of Valerie. Our hearts were broken for her. Every morning I called her, and every morning I prayed to say the right thing. Valerie put on a good front, smiling and efficiently handling funeral arrangements. But she was in shock and I knew it. During our conversations I tried to listen to her, reinforcing God's kindly ways.

I got out of bed and stood in front of the mirror, running my fingers through my hair. Wrinkles sagged above my eyelids and my eyes were puffy from grieving. I hadn't slept well, but that wasn't unusual. My sleep patterns had been skewed all my life, and I often got up during the night. No matter what time I went to bed, I'd wake every morning between 2:45 and 3:00 a.m.

Even as a baby, I remember standing in my crib when my father came home from a gig with the band. My mother slept in the bedroom across the hall from me, unaware I was awake. My hands clutched the crib rails as I peered into the darkness. My father would climb the stairs, flick on the hall light, turn toward the nursery, and see me standing there. He'd walk toward me, speaking in one of his many character impersonation voices. "What's this, Diane? You're still awake?"

I'd release my hands from the crib railing, my arms encircling his neck in a hug.

One night Dad held something behind his back. "I've got something for you," he said, bringing it out to show me. It was a little doll, unmovable and hard to the touch, different from my Sweetie Pie doll. It wore no clothes and had a fixed grin on its face and large eyes looking to one side.

"It's a Kewpie." Dad turned the doll over in my hands. "See its little wings?"

Now in my early fifties, I stood in front of the bathroom mirror recalling that three-year old moment, my daydream so vivid it felt as if the doll were in my hands again.

The alarm clock began to buzz. I turned it off and headed downstairs for my tea and my morning chat with Valerie. I took a sip of the weak tea, pressing the telephone buttons. "Hi, honey. How are you this morning?"

"Okay, Mom, but I have something to tell you," she replied. "This morning I stood in front of the bathroom mirror nude, washing, when I heard all-male voices singing in harmony. It sounded like the Marine Corps choir singing that old spiritual, *Swing Low, Sweet Chariot*."

I could hardly contain myself. "Oh Valerie, Luke's with my dad! I can just see it. There's a large room with many columns. A ledge circles the room with cherubs sitting on it. My dad is in the choir, and Luke sits above him, playing a little harp. He's throwing his head back, laughing. My mother is there, too. She's a greeter."

"But, Mom," Valerie interrupted, "why that song?"

"Val, do you know the words to that song? The message is in the words. Listen:

'I looked over Jordan and what did I see, comin' for to carry me home . . .' Valerie, Luke didn't have one, two, or even three angels.

---

[7] Psalms 91:4 - He shall cover thee with his feathers, and under his wings shall thou trust: his truth shall be thy shield and buckler.

He had a band of angels to carry him home.[7] And now he's with my parents. They've found each other," I exclaimed, believing every word.

"But, Mom, don't you think they could pick a better time to sing to me? I was washing myself without any clothes on." Her embarrassment surfaced in her slight laugh.

"Angels don't care if you're dressed or not. They're interested in your soul. And helping you. You received a blessing from God. How beautiful, honey. They're trying to make Luke's death less painful for you."

"There's only one person who knows how I feel."

"Who, Val?"

She replied without hesitation. "Auntie Dot, and she's dead."

I reflected for a moment, remembering Auntie Dot had lost her baby, too.

"They took my baby away," Val said, choking on her words.

"Val, we have only so many months, days, and minutes on earth. Luke's time was up. Jesus didn't want to hurt you. He loves you. Luke is with Him. I don't know why He took Luke so soon, either. Would it have been better at three years old? Or twenty or thirty? God knows what He's doing." I spoke calmly; a tear rolled down my cheek. I pressed my lips tightly together for I, too, nearly choked on my words. With a deep breath, I glanced at the kitchen clock. "Listen, Val, I've got to hang up and get ready for work. I'll talk to you tomorrow."

"Thanks for helping me find the right words," I said aloud as I hung up the phone and walked across the kitchen.

Gee, I thought, I didn't hear a choir of angels, and I'm supposed to be the spiritual one. Well, Valerie *is* his mother, I told myself.

As I climbed the stairs to the bedroom, I felt truly moved by God's angelic intervention for Valerie. Now she was forever awake. Like me, she could hear the angels.

The following Monday, I called Valerie at work, her first day back since Luke's death.

"Do you remember," she said, "when I called you to tell you I was home from work because Luke was sick? After we talked, about ten in the morning, I took him into his bedroom to change his diaper. He looked so sick, but for the first time that morning, he turned his head and looked over my shoulder. I said to him, 'Luke, are you looking at your angel'?"

"Valerie," I interrupted. I was shocked, remembering how I'd shouted back into the house that morning. "Uriel. He was there."

Valerie continued in a low tone. "Luke turned back and his eyes rolled up. He looked so sick." She paused. "If I . . . maybe if I . . .'"

"Val!" I stopped her. "You're blaming yourself. Don't do that."

"I can't help it, Mom, do you blame me?"

"No, it's not your fault." I tried to soothe her, concerned that I had to get ready for work again. "Please don't do this to yourself. I'll call you again later."

She's so down. I hated ending the phone call. I walked across the kitchen, and then turned around and called Val's work number again.

"Valerie, I just had to call you back. The doctor couldn't see how sick Luke was the night before. He's a professional and even he didn't know that something was seriously wrong. When I sent my angel Uriel over, the same angel who saved my life, he couldn't save Luke. Valerie, Luke was God's child. Uriel couldn't save him because he wasn't supposed to. That's all I wanted to say, honey. I have to go now."

"Bye, Mom. Thanks for calling back," she said.

When I hung up, the silence was enormous. The house had been quiet all morning. I climbed the stairs to the master bedroom. Without warning, I heard a hundred-voice choir singing an aria, a heavenly sound beyond description. Joy filled my heart to the very depths of my soul.

"I hear you!" In a rough, asthmatic voice, I sang back to them. *"Glory be to the Father and to the Son and to the Holy Ghost. As it was in the beginning, it is now and ever shall be, world without end, Amen."*

Even though I felt ashamed my voice wasn't as beautiful as it once was, instinctively I knew Heaven could hear only my soul singing.

The King of Kings stood in our midst, imprinting His song on our hearts. In the coming months, He continued to reassure, help, and heal us with His love.

Chapter Eighteen: Little Snowflake

Heaven arrives in the scent of roses

On Thanksgiving of 1993, Valerie invited Lloyd and me to attend Luke's memorial service at the hospital on December 5. I thought a moment and told her I believed the service was only for her and Mark. "But thanks for asking us," I replied, and left it at that.

The next night I dreamed of Luke. He crouched on his hands and knees on the rug of our family room. Those big, blue eyes looked directly at me, his head tilted back, laughing that silent laugh of his. The dream woke me from a sound sleep.

In the morning, I called Valerie to tell her that I'd go to the memorial service.

"I said you could go," she responded.

"I had a dream about Luke last night."

"What kind of dream?" It was strange she'd ask, because it's usually the other way around.

"Oh, just the way I'll always picture us together." I said.

He looked like a little cherub on the family room floor, laughing with his head thrown back, I thought.

"He was looking at me. That's all I remember. He wants me to be there." Then I told her, "I can go, but I'm sorry, honey, Dad won't be able to. His mother needs help."

"Meet us at our house, and we'll drive together."

The evening of the memorial service, a chilly night during the first week of December, the three of us climbed into Mark's black Blazer. Valerie sat directly behind the passenger seat so it was easier for me to get into the truck.

I glanced over at Mark as he drove. Such a nice young man, tall, full of good humor, always trying to please Valerie. Then I noticed a photograph of Valerie and Luke on the visor, one I'd not seen before. I carefully took it down to see it better.

"Mark likes that one of us together." Valerie moved up behind me and peered over my shoulder.

As I slipped the picture back into its place, I could see the hospital ahead. Mark pulled into the parking lot and took a spot under the light.

"I smell roses," I said.

Valerie pulled up behind me again. "Mark! I smell roses, too. Do you smell them?"

"Yes," he said softly.

"Do you have air freshener in here?"

"No."

"I still smell them," I said.

We got out of the Blazer and headed toward the hospital for the service. Valerie and Mark walked a step or two ahead of me.

"My God, there are roses all around me!" Valerie yelled.

I could picture our little Luke, flying at nose level, leading us into the hospital's memorial service. The fragrance of roses filled the hospital corridor and led us directly to the chapel on the main level. As we entered, the scent left us. Inside, soft flute and guitar music played. One of the five liturgists gave the parents of each deceased child a candle with their child's name on it. A golden snowflake too, as a remembrance from the child to the parents. The speaker told parents and family members they wanted to give us a symbol and decided on a snowflake because each one is uniquely different and they don't last long.

During the week of the memorial service, my cousin Eileen sent a poem for Valerie, one Auntie Dot wrote after she'd lost her infant son. After I read the words expressing my aunt's grief, I placed the poem inside my purse to give to Valerie the next time I saw her.

A week before Christmas, Lloyd and I bought a small Christmas tree for Luke's grave. I decorated it with a garland of golden stars and topped it with a single star of gold. Stars seemed appropriate. Luke was up there among the galaxies of gleaming stars God created. Because of my deep love of God and my spiritual beliefs, I accepted that everything in life has a purpose.

I placed a single ornament in the branches of the tree, a golden baby boy, then adjusted the branches to hold it in place against the strong winter winds. The following day I drove to the cemetery. As I parked the car at the curb, I smelled roses. I turned off the car's engine. "Luke, are you waiting for your Christmas gift?" I asked aloud. It wasn't the little red car I had planned to give him this Christmas. This gift was special, like he was.

The scent of roses triggered memories of Auntie Dot's poem. I retrieved the poem from my purse and picked up the little decorated tree sitting beside me. I stood outside the car watching the snow fall. As I looked up into the sky and let snowflakes dot my face, one caught on an eyelash. I blinked, and it was gone. I lowered my head and started walking toward Luke's grave, hearing only the crunch of my boots in the snow. I stood in front of the little grave. Removing my glove, I bent over and placed the small tree into the snow.

In that brief moment between thought and prayer, I remembered how Auntie Dot composed and read poems to family members on their birthdays or special occasions. Rising slowly, I stood in front of the tiny grave and softly whispered, "This is for you, sweetheart, from Auntie Dot."

A dream was dreamed of a sweet wild rose
Planted by God's own hand,
To blossom and bloom in this world of ours,
Oh, how can we understand?
The rose grew sweet with sorrow and pain,
Kept pure by God's own hand
'Til the time was right to adorn the throne
And join the angels' band.
In this garden on earth where flowers grow,
We choose in our simple way,

127

The sweetest and best of all the blossoms
Within our homes to stay.
So God in His infinite wisdom
Has plucked this rose so sweet
To adorn His throne in heaven
And gather close to his feet.

I held out my hand to the falling snowflakes and watched each one fall into my palm. I felt their tiny sting and closed my hand, rubbing them with my fingers. When I opened my hand, they had disappeared, leaving only a teardrop in their place.

"Merry Christmas, sweetheart. We'll always love you."

I turned and slowly walked back to the car. The scent of roses had disappeared. One little snowflake perched on my lip. It seemed so light and delicate as I licked it away. A kiss for Grandma from Luke, I thought.

The Lord of Lords seemed to be everywhere for Valerie, Mark, and me. Our lives changed; God had touched us with His awesome work. Christ's teachings were destined to increase Valerie's spiritual gifts.

CHAPTER NINETEEN: VALERIE'S ENLIGHTENMENT

Accept the truth of your visions

When Luke had been gone three months, I received a call from Valerie. Extremely excited, she said, "Mom, oh, Mom, I had a vision tonight."

"A vision? What was it like?"

"I was ready for bed and praying, asking for protection in the white light of God, as I do every night. I asked to hold Luke one more time. All of a sudden, I was holding Luke under this very bright beam of light. The light was so bright you could feel the power in it. Luke was completely naked except for little wings coming out of his back. The wings looked like they were budding . . ."

"Luke had wings?" I exclaimed, interrupting her. *A cherub.*

"Yes! I turned him slightly, and I could see them. They were small, like little flower buds. The entire time it felt as if I was watching a movie. But I was really holding him. He was grabbing at my blouse. I thought, I'm not supposed to be doing this, you're dead."

"The experience felt real, Mom. As I asked myself why this was happening, Luke flew out of my arms. When I went to look for him, he was with Grandma and Grandpa Tillman. Grandma held Luke, and his arms were going up and down. Remember? He always did that when he was excited. Grandma looked fat and healthy in her green dress. Grandpa sat next to her, wearing his blue suit. Grandma Verda and Grandpa Harry stood just a little behind them, and I could see your Grandma

Verda didn't have her crutch. Grandpa Harry wore a gray shirt, but I couldn't see what color slacks he had on. Mark's grandmother wore a dress and sweater. She stood away from everyone, but she was there. Many people were standing behind our family, but I couldn't tell who they were. When I was leaving, they all waved and smiled at me. I waved and smiled back."

I felt uplifted. "Oh, Val, Luke's found the family. I knew it. I just knew it."

"You know," Valerie confided, "every night I prayed to God to please let me hold Luke again. Mom, God let me hold him. He let me hold him one more time."

Eventually the angelic interventions, celestial choirs, awareness of a presence, and the fragrant scents slowed in frequency. I knew God had sent these blessings filled with love to reassure us of His presence, to support and heal us. We were all given the unforgettable experience of knowing Luke's death had a purpose, and learned to not fear life or death because all things are set by God's divine hand.

The experiences led Valerie to discovery and fulfillment. Her spirituality was awakened, and she would never be quite the same again. Nor would I. God chose me to share these blessings with Valerie. I was in awe that because of these blessings I had a deeper inner connection with God. I became conscious of true symmetry and my beliefs came into a perfect balance. My life finally had a meaning. I was filled with a deep, instinctive knowledge that God's interventions guided me toward my next higher step.

As I became attuned with the other dimension, my angel encouraged my talents. My life changed. Even as God has given others a special job to do, He had also given one to me. I became inspired to write about these experiences.

There was no way I could not write about it. I truly believe my gifts developed so I could share this with others. Without realizing it, I began to surpass my own expectations. I wasn't afraid, for even though I lived on this side of Heaven, I knew Heaven was on my side.

I know that many people in the world aren't listening to God. The Virgin's message about helping her Son reach the world has failed to touch everyone. Icons cry, rosaries turn to gold, people have visions, and we still don't listen. God sends His angels to Valerie, me, and others so we, through our experiences, can help change the world.

In the six months following Luke's death, Valerie confided in her friends about the spiritual blessings God bestowed on her and Mark, but they always found logical explanations for them. They were conditioned all their lives to ignore such signs or to think of them as symptoms of a nervous breakdown. Her friends did everything they could to discount Valerie's spiritual experiences and divert her attention away from them.

Valerie spoke of flying to California to visit with James Van Praagh, a gifted psychic medium and spiritual counselor.

"With all the spiritual blessings God has sent you, do you think the trip is necessary?" I asked her.

Without hesitation, Valerie told me, "Mom, you're the only one I can talk to. When I mention sights, smells, visions, and sounds, people think I've gone off the deep end. They don't understand. They don't want to hear about it."

Val read *Embraced by the Light* by Betty Eadie and George Anderson's book, *Our Children Forever,* over and over. As the months went by, she started giving copies of these books to anyone who had lost a child. In this way, helping others with their loss became her therapy, as well.

Sadly, parents never completely recover from the death of a child. They always remember their child's birthday and date of death. At Christmas and other holidays, parents constantly wonder, what would my child look like now? The pain feels unbearable, decreasing only in the sense it becomes a silent companion. For Valerie and Mark, the shock of Luke's death ended and the hard realization of it set in after the first six months.

Many marriages fail after a child's death. The partners' reaction to grief can be so different they cannot understand one another. Many men channel grief through physical activity. They're taught to ignore or suppress emotion. When a woman cries about her child's death, men often feel so uncomfortable they leave the area where grief is strong. They go to a bar, get involved in sports, or perhaps go out and pull weeds. At first, after Luke's death, Mark had a hard time dealing with it, and he didn't realize there were significant differences between his and Valerie's grieving processes. With this new understanding, that their reactions were simply different, their marriage remained strong.

In the months after Luke's death, Valerie found it difficult to sleep. Years ago, when I had the heavy responsibility of caring for my mother, I'd been no match for Valerie's mood swings. I asked Barbara Allen if she'd counsel her after Luke's death, and thanks to her "love boxes" and cassettes of encouragement, Valerie began meditating again and took control of her life.

"Before you become the butterfly," Barbara Allen told her on a tape, "you have to go through many metamorphoses." She explained that by using meditation, Valerie could go anywhere in the world.

As she grieved over Luke, Valerie went to the ocean in her mind because of its calming effect. The inner sounds of waves and surf soothed her. Once there, she'd sit on a large rock and wait for Jesus. As the weeks went by, she saw Him sitting on the rock, waiting for her to arrive. Then they'd sit together, watching the sunset. He'd hold her in His arms as she fell asleep.

Since Luke's death, Valerie's dreams hadn't been as plentiful as they'd once been, and we seldom spoke of them. Then, on one of my visits I noticed a beautiful Lenox china figurine displayed on the piano in the living room. I picked it up, turned it over, and read its title: "The Children's Blessing."

Val looked over my shoulder. "Do you remember the dream I had? Of Jesus sitting on a large rock holding Luke? There were fifty or more children around Him. Jesus looked as He does in pictures, with long hair, a beard, and a white robe. He seemed to be conducting an orientation for the children. As He pointed to each child, I heard Him say, 'Now, we each have to take care of our wings'."

Happy for her, I said, "What a beautiful dream."

"You know, Mom, I always asked God, why Luke? Why not the baby of someone who didn't care about her child?" She paused, then continued. "And I always wondered what Luke was doing, how he got along in Heaven. God answered my prayer, didn't He?" After a moment, she added, "Mom, could you analyze the dream for me?"

"Well, Val, analyzing a dream amounts to what you feel when considering the symbols in the dream. What they mean to you personally. It's your dream, not mine."

"But you're better at it than I am. Please?" she begged.

"But I may look at the dream differently than you would."

"That's okay. I still want to hear what you think."

"First of all, Val, this dream is very spiritual and sent directly from Heaven. Next, consider that Jesus was sitting on a rock. The rock is the symbol of his church. Since you noticed his long hair, this could indicate strength, like the story of Samson and Delilah in the Old Testament. You say He's holding Luke on his lap and guiding the other children gathered around. This may mean He's personally taking care of Luke and all the other children. And what did He say?"

"He said, 'Now, we each have to take care of our wings'."

"Right. The children with him have wings, and since angels are messengers, the wings could indicate a message. The message is that all children are cared for by the greatest Teacher of all time, the Son of God. There is no need to worry about Luke. He's learning with all the other little angels about wings and other things in Heaven."

A few nights later, Valerie phoned me from her home. "Mom, do you remember when you removed the spirit of someone who didn't belong in my apartment? Well, there's something in my house." Her voice sounded nervous. "I can't see it the way I saw the girl in my apartment, but I know it's evil. It's trying to get at me telepathically."

"Last night I was reading about the resurrection of Christ in the Bible. When I came to the part where Mary looks for Christ near the tomb, something crossed my mind that was so evil. I began thinking; did Jesus and Mary have a sexual relationship? Mom, how could I have a thought like that? I told the Evil One to get away from me. Could you come over here and get rid of it for me? I know it's hiding somewhere."

"Valerie, you can get rid of it yourself. You know how, with prayer in the name of Jesus Christ. It wouldn't hurt when you're offering up your prayer to light a white candle which symbolizes the purity of Our Lord and a blue candle, which signifies Christ, the sky, the oceans, and the universe."

"But I feel like your strength is stronger than mine. I'm afraid. Please come over, please?"

"Okay, honey, I'm on my way. Remember what we discussed once, that evil has a way of finding you when you're emotionally down?"

Only to make your life worse, I added to myself.

When I arrived at Valerie's home, I took the blue candle into each room as I prayed. Feeling confident, we improved upon the ritual I'd used years ago and walked into each room unafraid. Valerie followed me with holy water, sprinkling each room in our quest to clear out the evil spirit.

We finished all the rooms except Luke's nursery. As I opened the door, a light breeze came from within. The flame flickered as I continued praying. Without warning, a cold breeze touched my face as the evil spirit left the room.

We returned to the kitchen and sat down. I asked Valerie to hold my hands as we said the Lord's Prayer together.

After we said the final "Amen," Valerie asked, "What do you think, Mom?"

"There was something of an evil nature there. Even the hairs on the back of my neck stood on end. But you have a clean house again, Val. You would think the Evil One knows us by now and we wouldn't be bothered by him, but I guess it'll never stop."

I paused and thought for a moment. "By now, I know you realize there's a relationship between the spiritual and sexuality. This is something the Evil One takes advantage of to enter the consciousness of a person. He used it tonight, interrupting your thoughts as you read the Bible, didn't he?"

"Yes, I get it. But isn't his power a little subtle?"

"That's the whole point. It's unrecognizable. It seems to be merely a passing thought. He uses this kind of thing all the time." Smiling at her, I added, "And you caught him at it!"

"Mom, why don't people get rid of evil?"

"Well, Val, they may not understand what's happening. Also, people don't know how to get rid of evil because they think it originated within them. And if they tried to get rid of it, they might not know enough to use all levels of spirituality. The lesson is to distinguish the difference between good and evil. Once they understand where it comes from, they don't allow it and get rid of it with prayer."

"You lost me there, Mom! I don't understand what you mean."

"I've found there are several levels of spirituality, Val. You could refer to three of them as the religious, metaphysical, and intuitive levels. I use a combination of these levels to conquer evil."

"And people don't realize that putting them together is important?"

"Each of us looks for our own spirituality in different ways. Most people don't even know what the word *metaphysical* means. It's hard to understand when philosophy goes beyond reason. Interpretation of dreams and candle color meanings are both based on theory, not fact. The intuitive level is knowing through feelings, not with the mind. Val, you used intuition tonight when you felt something in the nursery and called me. The religious level uses prayer and church doctrine for protection. The evil spirit you felt in the nursery was eager to take advantage of your grief. Praying is the only way to break this hold and free ourselves from lower influences that cause evil. Prayer can break addiction, habits, and weaknesses within us. Tonight, we went after evil with a combination of ritual and prayer." I paused and Valerie leaned toward me, listening intently.

"We used the metaphysical level—taking the blue candle and holy water from room to room, the religious level—reciting the Lord's Prayer, and the intuitive level—sensing the cold breeze as the evil spirit left. All of these levels work in forming a belief system. By using them together, we protected your spiritual growth."

"But what about other people?" Valerie looked puzzled. "How can they find out about all this?"

"This is something they have to learn for themselves. But as time goes by, they'll learn more and more about it. It's a quest for a higher level of spirituality. All the time, this treasure is right in front of them, waiting to be discovered."

My experience in guiding Valerie's spiritual growth led me to help and heal others through Christ's eternal love.

Chapter Twenty: The Spiritual Healings

Work with natural energies

I'd just left a patient's room at the hospital when my petite, pretty co-worker Jodi approached me in the corridor. Her winning manner fit the typical recreational therapist. With an engaging smile, she motioned at me to join her in the day room.

Jodi had been dieting the past few weeks because her wedding date was near. "Don't ever let anyone tell you that your aches and pains will go away if you lose weight," she said in a disappointed voice. "I thought if I lost a few pounds, the pain in my knee would disappear. It didn't. You know, I haven't been able to put any pressure on it for years, and now it's *really* hurting me. I need surgery, but it's too late to recuperate before the wedding."

I patted her arm. "Oh, Jodi."

"Boy, is your hand hot. Touch my arm again, Diane. It's much cooler than your hand."

"Yes, I can feel the difference. Jodi, years ago I learned to transfer pain out of the body."

"Oh, do it! Get rid of the pain," she begged.

"You have to believe you can let go of it," I told her softly.

"I believe, I believe!"

"Close your eyes and imagine the pain shooting out of the back of your knee." I stooped down and grasped her knee carefully but firmly

137

while I closed my eyes. I imagined the pain shooting out the back of her knee. A minute or two passed. When I removed the pressure from her knee with my hand, it gave her the clue to release the thought of pain there. I did the same. Then we both opened our eyes. "Did you visualize the pain leaving?"

"Yes," she said. "What now?"

"We'll have to see what happens," I said. She hurried from the dayroom to continue her rounds.

The next day I saw Jodi on the rehabilitation unit at the hospital. "How do you feel?" I asked.

"You know, there's no pain in my knee. Nothing. When I told you 'I believe,' I only half-believed you," she said sheepishly. "But it's fine now. Do you suppose the pain will come back?"

I thought for a moment. What could I tell her? Fear of rejection often led me to conceal my true feelings. I couldn't bring myself to explain to her that God, through my angel, was with me. I believed that, but would she? So I replied, "If it does, imagine the pain leaving your knee again. Concentrate and believe."

"Thanks, Di," Jodi said with a big grin.

"You're going to have a great wedding day." I smiled back at her. As I started down the corridor toward my unit, there was no doubt in my mind that something had changed. A feeling of spiritual contentment filled my heart. I, too, was amazed.

Six months after Luke died, the devotional services I'd been conducting at the hospital changed. I shared with my patients the miracle that the Virgin of Guadalupe had given to my grandmother, helping her walk again. I explained how my lungs had shut down and how my angel intervened, telling me I wasn't going to die. I started teaching my patients how to pray using the Bible's Twenty-third Psalm.

"I'm not going to pray to Jesus for you. You're going to pray to Him yourselves," I told them firmly but gently. "You're going to see Jesus by the still waters. He told us He'd be with us always. As you sit here in your wheelchairs, feel yourself walking beside Him. Feel His arm around you, or His hand holding yours. Jesus said that if you believe, He will answer your prayers. He didn't say you'd be perfect. My grandmother wasn't perfect, but she walked. My own health isn't perfect. I have asthma, and I lived. When you get to the end of the prayer, I want you to visualize yourselves in the house of the Lord with Jesus standing next to you. He's there. As a child looks up to his father, ask Him to help you."

As I sat at the table with my patients, I turned around to the stereo system for a moment, searching for a musical background for the Twenty-third Psalm. I started the music and faced the patients. "Now close your eyes and believe Jesus is waiting for you. See it."

The minutes went by. The music stopped automatically, and we all sat in silence around the table, asking Jesus to help us. As I opened my eyes, I asked, "Did anyone see Him?"

A few nodded, and then one of the female patients said, "Yes, I was there. I saw Jesus, an angel, and the Blessed Virgin. I saw all three of them."

"Beautiful, just beautiful." I smiled, looking at her sitting across the table, which covered her amputated legs.

"Forty years ago, the pastor of my church gave me the Twenty-third Psalm at my confirmation. It's there for you, too. Always use it when you pray. I'm not a healer, but I believe the power of God is within and works through us. As I touch you, believe, and your faith will heal you."

I put on the music to *The Lord's Prayer*. After the first few bars of music, I rose. The patient to my left sat in his wheelchair, shaking. I leaned forward, and put my arms around him. I told him Jesus was with him, that he would feel better soon. As my arms encircled him, I felt my hands warming and couldn't seem to let go. I picked up one of his trembling hands and held it. As his shaking decreased, tears filled my eyes and rolled down my cheeks.

The African-American lady across the table felt so inspired by what she saw that she raised her arms to the ceiling. "Praise the Lord, oh, praise the Lord!"

As I turned to the next patient, a nurse's aide walked into the room. She stood there for a moment, trying to grasp what was happening. The secretary from the nurses' station entered the room also, and stood near the end of the table. She stood, unmoving, until I laid my hands on her, for I sensed that she needed strength in her life. Still crying, I hugged her. I moved from patient to patient, around the table to the lady who had raised her arms. "I'm sorry, I don't know your name," I said to her.

"My name is Evelyn," she told me. "I have lupus."

"You'll feel better soon. Jesus is with you. He has always been with you." I touched her arm, then bending down I touched my cheek to hers.

The music ended, and it was silent once more. "Thank you for coming to our devotional service today. I hope you liked it. It's lunchtime now. Please feel free to join the other patients."

Some of the patients left, while others remained in the recreation room. I walked over to them, smiling. The amputee patient moved her wheelchair over to me. "That was truly inspirational. Thank you and God bless you."

Feeling the truth of her words, I replied simply, "He already has."

Another patient said, "I believed everything you said. And I don't know if you realize this, but I saw little twinkling lights around your head."

"Oh, thank you for telling me."

As Evelyn moved her wheelchair toward the doorway, she stopped in front of me. "I wasn't going to come to your service," she admitted. "I've been depressed about my illness. I'm so glad I came. I feel better already."

I walked over to the sink, thinking how important it was to wash my hands after giving a spiritual healing. I had discovered that hand washing not only prevented infections and illnesses in the hospital, but it also dissolved the transfer of negative energy that made the patient sick in the first place.

Years earlier, I'd released an energy transference that had given me a great deal of pain. Through this experience, I realized healing energy exists in each of us. I refer to this invisible energy as the "health light." This aura of healing energy surrounds each person with a glow of various colors. This energy has the ability to pass out of the body and can also draw other energies into the body.

At times, I'm able to see the energy surrounding others because I have a heightened level of sensitivity. After giving a spiritual healing, I've seen the flow of my own energy leave my fingertips in a sparkling, white stream of radiant light. I call this energy the "light of God," for

I believe it is directly given by Him. It comes from within. The light is what we are in God's sight and is true soul power.

Shaking the excess water from my hands, I took a paper towel from the dispenser. I thought about yesterday's activity class when I'd asked the patients to imagine all their illnesses leaving their body though their fingertips. "The mind controls the body. Today I want you to get well by thinking well."

One patient looked directly at me. "I believe that."

I nodded and smiled at her, then turned to the others. "Okay, everyone, imagine that you have just thrown a baseball into the air. Imagine all your illnesses leaving through your fingertips as you release the ball. See the illness leaving you. It's leaving. I see it leaving you. That's right; you're doing it. Just imagine."

When I finished washing my hands, there were three patients still in the room. Only Emily could talk. I sat down beside her. During our conversation, she whispered, "Who is that man standing behind you?" I turned and looked around, but no one was there.

"Oh, him," I said, turning back to her, "that's my guardian angel. He's always with me. I feel his presence more when I'm at the hospital or when I'm sick. He saved my life a few times." I wasn't surprised at her question, only that she saw him. I knew he was there.

Emily died three days later, unexpectedly, from a heart attack. I realized then why she could see my angel.

❦

I sensed the incredible presence of Christ when I touched others during spiritual healings. Next, I'd understand that He plans everything for the good of those who love Him.

Chapter Twenty-One: At Heaven's Doorway

Fulfill your spiritual purpose with Heaven's guidance

In 1994, a year and a half after Luke's death, I entered our dark kitchen, turned on the light over the table, and sat down. For the better part of the evening I'd been upstairs in the den, writing. I felt as if I were on a higher spiritual level than ever before. I'd reached a level of sensitivity others did not perceive in me. Blessed by the celestial dimension, I knew it was time to share my heart, soul, and mind.

I pulled one of the chairs closer so I could put my legs up. Tired, I rested an elbow on the table, rubbed my eyes, and pinched the bridge of my nose with my fingers. I lifted my head and leaned it on my knuckles. As I stared into the kitchen, a thin crack in the atmosphere formed. A small foot and then a leg appeared on the kitchen floor. A small hand held the side of the opening. A tranquil feeling came over me as I gazed at Heaven's doorway. I blinked then blinked again. I sat straight up, removing my legs from the chair and placed both feet on the floor.

"Grandma," he said in a child's soft voice.

"Luke, you're here."

"Yes, Grandma. You love me, Grandma?"

"Yes, sweetheart, I love you. Luke, you can talk!"

"Yes, I can."

"Do you have wings, honey?"

Luke turned around and I saw two little wings.

"Do you fly, sweetheart?"

"No, Grandma, I don't fly." Luke appeared older, perhaps two years old. He flew up and hovered, fluttering his wings like a butterfly. I realized his small wings couldn't support him.

"Is anyone with you, Luke? Is Grandpa there?" I asked, referring to my dad.

"Yes, Grandpa's here."

"Does Grandpa have wings?"

"No, Grandma. Grandpa doesn't have wings."

"What does Grandpa do, Luke?"

"Grandpa sings in the choir."

"What does Grandma do?"

"She watches."

"Luke, do you play a musical instrument?"

"Yes." He didn't know or couldn't pronounce the name of the instrument. Telepathically, I had the impression it was a stringed instrument.

"Do you have a playmate there?"

"I play with Gary."

"Does Gary have wings, too?"

"Yes, Grandma, he does." Intuitively, I knew Gary was Auntie Dot's son who died at six months of age over fifty years ago.

"Auntie Dot feels bad that Mama lost me, Grandma. Tell Mama not to worry. I'm happy here. I see Jesus. It wasn't anybody's fault. It was my time. I'm in your book, huh, Grandma."

My eyes filled with tears. "Yes, sweetheart, you're in my book."

"Everybody is so happy you're writing about them. You're going to tell the whole world about all of us, huh, Grandma?"

"Yes, sweetheart, I am."

Luke said nothing more. I saw his hand on the doorway from which he'd appeared. Slowly he stepped back into the thin crack, fading into the other dimension.

I remembered the first time Luke made his presence known to me, six months after his death, on his first birthday. That afternoon, as I lay relaxing on the sofa in our family room, thoughts of him began to surface. I wondered if he could walk and if he were taller. As I thought about Luke, he materialized through a crack in the air. He was scantily dressed, wearing only a heavy cloth diaper making him appear bow-legged, his feet turned slightly inward.

Luke stood on the long white runners leading into the kitchen. He modeled for me, showing me he could walk. When Luke turned and walked on a white runner back to the opening, I recalled a movie clip my father had taken of me outside Grandma Verda's house when I was a toddler. Just as I thought that, Luke turned his head and disappeared at Heaven's doorway with a smile.

Luke reappeared several more times, although the apparitions were not as vivid. Like a short clip from a movie, each appearance provided me with a new piece of information about his development. Every time, I noticed he was growing, learning, and developing a personality. I realized then that the Lord had given him a special job to do. He allowed Luke's spirit to return to us briefly, whenever our hearts needed comforting.

One afternoon in late September of that same year, Valerie stopped in. "Mom, I think I'm pregnant," she said softly.

"Oh, Val, I'm so happy for you." Perhaps now a new life would ease the pain of losing Luke.

As the weeks went by, I wondered what effect her grieving might have on the new life within her. The anniversary of Luke's death was approaching when she phoned me at home. "Mom, I'm bleeding heavily, and the doctor told me to stay off my feet for a few days."

"Honey, I'll take off work to help you. The same thing happened to me when I carried you, and it's frightening."

The next morning I arrived at Valerie's home. She stretched out on the sofa and I sat across from her on the matching blue loveseat. We talked most of the day while I made her bed, did some laundry, and planned dinner. Val turned on the television in the beautiful oak entertainment center that Mark had crafted for them. How talented they both are, I thought.

It was nearing lunchtime. When I brought sandwiches into the living room, Val was watching a talk show that didn't appeal to me. But when I glanced at the television a second time, for one split second, my eyes caught a glimpse of a dark, paper thin, small figure stepping out from behind the entertainment center. I could see it clearly against the light-colored wall. The little figure peered at me with its large eyes, surprised that I noticed it. It ran quickly across the wall like a silhouette. It reminded me of one of my father's old Betty Boop cartoons. I looked over at Valerie but said nothing.

One day in late February of '95, Valerie left work early with cramps. I called her the following day. "Hi, Val, how are you?"

"Okay. Better. But the doctor said I should get off my feet again." She was silent, then, "Mom?"

"Yes?"

"I saw a small, shadowy figure almost like an animated cartoon run into the nursery this morning."

"It's Luke, honey. I saw his shadow behind the entertainment center when I came over to take care of you. A little figure, paper thin, peeked out from behind your entertainment center and looked at me with large eyes. I didn't tell you at the time because I didn't want to upset you."

"But, Mom, why is he coming around?"

"Val, each time he appeared, you were sick and told by the doctor to stay off your feet. It seems Luke is the new baby's guardian angel."

"Ooooooh," she said with new understanding.

"He'll always be there for you, honey, our little Luke."

"Mom," Valerie paused slightly, "did Grandpa ever sing the song *Because*?"

"Yes, he sang *Because* at weddings. Why?"

"I keep hearing that song. Do you know the words?"

I smiled to myself, for in a sense history had repeated itself. "Yes, Val, it's an old favorite, and the message is loud and clear."

I glanced at the doorway and reflected a moment on the golden rose in my near-death experience. Each corner of my heart filled with emotion. Christ had stood beside His mother and me, speaking words of thanksgiving and new hope for the world. I remembered the words, all the words, and my father's golden voice singing *Because*.

BECAUSE

(1902) *Music by Guy d'Hardelot, English lyrics by Edward Teschemacher*

Because you come to me with naught save love,
And hold my hand and lift mine eyes above,
A wider world of hope and joy I see,
Because you come to me.

Because you speak to me in accent sweet,
I find the roses waking 'round my feet,
And I am led through tears and joy to thee
Because you speak to me!

Because God made thee mine, I'll cherish thee
Through light and darkness through all time to be,
And pray His love may make our love divine,
Because God made thee mine!

EPILOGUE

Heaven's blessings are infinite

After Luke's death, Valerie and Mark held a birthday celebration for him every year on April 5 at a restaurant near their home.

"Meet us at the house, we'll go together. After dinner you're invited to come back for cake and ice cream," Valerie told Lloyd and me the week before Luke's sixth birthday celebration.

When we arrived at their home the following Friday, our three-and-a-half year old granddaughter, Alexis, met us at the front door.

"Grandma, Grandpa, come see what's next to Luke's tree," she said, taking my hand. After Luke died, Valerie and Mark planted a small apple tree outside, near their patio. They affectionately called it Luke's tree.

We walked through the kitchen, around the table Mark had handcrafted for their home before Luke was born. On the table sat a small frosted chocolate cake topped with a little fuzzy yellow duck.

I peered outside the sliding glass doors at the tree. In the branches were six yellow ribbons holding a fresh yellow mum.

Lexie looked up at us, then pointed outside. "See. See the ducks?" She pointed to a mated pair of mallard ducks sitting beneath Luke's tree.

"Oh, I see them," I exclaimed.

Valerie entered the kitchen from the hallway. "The ducks have been staring at the tree all day. Every year, they return on Luke's birthday."

We headed for the restaurant, one Mark and Valerie frequently patronized with Luke. The hostess sat the five of us at a table in the center of the room. After the waitress took our order, she began removing the empty sixth chair from the table.

"You can leave the extra chair there, it's okay," Val told her.

After the waitress left, she turned to me. "That always happens, no matter where we are. There's always the extra chair, the extra ticket or a song playing that reminds us of him. It's always like that."

During dinner, Mark told a humorous story to Lloyd about one of his friends. I sat at the far end of the table, hearing only pieces of the story. I glanced at Lexie, sitting across the table from me. She wouldn't drink her kiddy cocktail because a stem from the maraschino cherry stuck out of the glass. Valerie leaned over, plucked the cherry from Lexie's glass, and popped it into her mouth. With a gentle tug, she removed the stem protruding between her lips and smiled broadly at Lexie.

While the five of us celebrated Luke's birthday, Eric Clapton's *Tears in Heaven* played softly over the entertainment system. I peered at the empty chair across the table and smiled. In our hearts, it isn't empty at all, I thought.

Blessings from Heaven continue to grace Mark and Valerie. Six years after Lexie was born, they had another daughter, Tori. Each year they hold Luke's birthday celebration at their home. The restaurant they patronized with him, and later, our family, closed several years ago. Fourteen years after Luke's birth and death, the mallard ducks still visit on his birthday.

THE END

CHAPTER NOTES

Chapter 5: Portals of Dreams

1) El Mahdy, Christine. *Mummies, Myth and Magic*. New York: Thames and Hudson, 1989.

Chapter 6: Conquering Evil

2) *Heirloom Master Reference Edition Bible, Odd Fellows Edition, King James Version*. Wichita, Kansas: Devore & Sons, Inc., 1978, p. 453. Matthew 4:10. "Get thee hence, Satan, for it is written thou shalt worship the Lord thy God, and him only shalt thou serve."

Chapter 10: The Christmas Angel

3) Ibid, p. 310. Psalms 91:11-12. "For He shall give His angels charge over thee to keep thee in all thy ways. They shall bear thee up in their hands lest thou dash thy foot against a stone."

Chapter 11: A Job Well Done

4) Ibid, p. 452. Matthew 5:8. "Blessed are the pure in heart, for they shall see God."

5) Ibid, p. 453. Matthew 6:9-13. "After this manner therefore pray ye: 'Our Father which art in heaven, Hallowed be thy name. Thy

kingdom come. Thy will be done in earth, as it is in heaven. Give us this day our daily bread. Forgive us our debts, as we forgive our debtors. And lead us not into temptation, but deliver us from evil: For thine is the kingdom and the power and the glory, forever. Amen.'

Chapter 14: An Angel Among Us

6) Ibid, p. 78. Exodus 12:13. "And the blood shall be to you for a token upon the houses where ye are. And when I see the blood, I will pass over you, and the plague shall not be upon you to destroy you, when I smite the land of Egypt."

Chapter 17: Heartstrings from Heaven

7) Ibid, p. 310. Psalms 91:4. "He shall cover thee with his feathers, and under his wings shall thou trust: his truth shall be thy shield and buckler."

ABOUT THE AUTHOR

DIANE LINE is an active member of the Arizona Authors Association, Toastmasters International, and the Professional Writers of Prescott. A Chicago native, Diane and her husband Lloyd moved to Prescott, Arizona in 2002. Their daughter Valerie, son-in-law Mark, and two grandchildren, Alexis and Victoria, live in Illinois.

An inspirational writer, actor, director, counselor, hypnotherapist and metaphysician, Diane has appeared at speaking engagements with Toastmasters International, nursing homes, hospitals and other clubs and organizations.

Diane was raised in the Lutheran tradition and attended Zoar Lutheran School and Church in Elmwood Park, Illinois. She attended Luther North High School in Chicago, and graduated from Triton College in River Grove, Illinois with an Associate of Applied Science degree in Therapeutic Recreation Therapy. She also holds a Master of Arts degree in Metaphysics, the title Metaphysical Consultant, and a certificate in Hypnotherapy from the Academy of Advanced Thinking. She's listed in the 2007-2008 Cambridge Who's Who Directory of Executives, Professionals and Entrepreneurs.

For further information regarding her or *At Heaven's Doorway*, send a self-addressed, stamped envelope to:

Diane Line
P.O. Box 10754
Prescott, AZ 86304

E-mail may be forwarded to dianethewriter@yahoo.com
or visit Diane at Author's Den: www.authorsden.com/dianeline
Visit www.authorhouse.com or my web site at:
www.atheavensdoorway.com

Printed in the United States
141328LV00003B/15/P